WINE CLASS

JO BURZYNSKA

All you need to know about wine in New Zealand

RANDOM HOUSE
NEW ZEALAND

A RANDOM HOUSE BOOK published by Random House New Zealand
18 Poland Road, Glenfield, Auckland, New Zealand

For more information about our titles
go to www.randomhouse.co.nz

A catalogue record for this book is available
from the National Library of New Zealand

Random House New Zealand is part of the Random House Group
New York   London   Sydney   Auckland   Delhi   Johannesburg

First published 2009

© 2009 Jo Burzynska

The moral rights of the author have been asserted

ISBN 978 1 86979 100 1

Design: Kate Barraclough
Author photograph: Kurt Langer
Printed in Hong Kong

Contents

Introduction

I'd love to tell you about the vinous epiphany that turned me on to wine, but I can't. There simply wasn't one. Like most people who've come to be captivated by the greatness of the grape, there was no Eureka moment while wandering through a vineyard or drinking a mind-blowing glass of mature Burgundy.

I grew up in the eighties, and my early memories of wine were of straw-clad fiascos of thin Chianti and sickly sweet rosé poured from bulbous bottles that both made better candleholders than an introduction to the pleasures of wine. Unless you're very lucky, your first wine experience is often less than inspirational.

My first active foray into wine was not particularly propitious either. As a teenager I crafted my own noxious examples, which although prized by my peers garnered most of their acclaim for properties other than the fine aromas and flavours in which they were sadly lacking.

It wasn't until I went to university, that hotbed of alcoholic exploration, that I became aware that all wine was not the same. While many of my friends were still calculating the ratio of alcohol to price, I began to spend my meagre budget on as wide a variety of wine as possible.

Although there was a student wine society at my college, I felt way too intimidated to join. Seeing its members sashay across the quad in black ties and ball gowns, holding glasses filled from expensive-looking bottles, I didn't feel that I had the budget or the background to be part of this branch of bacchanalia.

I did eventually encounter a kindred spirit with whom I pooled funds to purchase my first case of wine. This watershed moment happened at an unstuffy and adventurous wine shop, where a clued-up member of staff quizzed us about our tastes and put together a great selection for us to work through.

Inspired by this experience, I signed up for an evening class in wine while studying for a Masters degree in English. Then, at the end of my academic course, instead of pursuing the PhD I'd originally planned, an advertisement in the newspaper for a relief manager in a funky forward-thinking wine chain attracted my attention and changed my career path irreversibly.

Soon I was running my own shop, studying for wine qualifications and revelling in being surrounded by a product that fascinated me. I got a huge buzz out of using my newfound knowledge to guide customers to discover wines they'd like and help them explore their individual tastes, much as that wine store employee had helped me.

Communicating about wine has remained the core of my work, especially once I progressed to the wine writing and editing that's been my job for the last decade. It's a journey that's taken me across the world to many winegrowing regions and one that led me from the UK, where it all began, to New Zealand, where I now live.

While my move may have meant giving up the stupendous selection of wines available to me in Britain, this has been more than compensated for by the excitingly youthful and dynamic wine industry that's now on my doorstep. Largely driven by passion rather than the pomposity that I had encountered in some sectors of the British wine trade, the people that I've encountered here are as refreshing as the wines they make.

Living in a wine-producing nation such as New Zealand offers invaluable resources for anyone interested in wine. From Kumeu River in the north to Felton Road in the south, there are many places making great wines that can be sampled in situ, an experience often enriched by liberal splashes of personal knowledge and enthusiasm.

I regularly travel up and down the country to glean information to share in my current role as wine editor for 'Viva', the *New Zealand Herald*'s lifestyle magazine, and through my Adventures in Wine school. This book is based on my 'Viva' columns and my wine classes both of which have provided me with plenty of feedback on what wine drinkers really want to know.

Wine Class not only explores the different elements that create the myriad tastes and textures in the wines found on the shelves of New Zealand's wine shops and restaurant wine lists, but also includes pointers to where the most exciting bottles can be sourced and how they're best enjoyed, plus plenty of tips to help you buy better.

As I discovered, one of the best ways to learn about wines is through tasting them, so at the end of every chapter I've recommended examples that illustrate the points made. Follow these tastings and by the end of the book you will have tried wines made from most of the key grape varieties and regions available in New Zealand today.

Wine Class offers a guided trip through the world of wine. I hope that it will inspire you to embark on many adventures of your own, equipped with the knowledge that should ensure these journeys are as exciting and enjoyable as mine.

CHAPTER ONE

Questions of Taste

'Wine is the simple distillation of time and place, from the auspices of a single idea, into a form that we can imbibe.'

Nick Mills, Rippon Vineyard, Central Otago

Wine is one of the world's most diverse and complex drinks, shaped as it is by a dizzying array of influences, from the grapes themselves, to the place and climate in which they are grown, to the people who make the wine. This creates some heady combinations, but it can also mean the learning journey can feel a little intimidating for those just starting out.

There's a greater choice available to the New Zealand wine drinker today than ever before, opening up exciting possibilities for completely new taste experiences that range from the first local wines made from the Austrian Grüner Veltliner grape through to the swelling selection of rich and succulent Spanish reds.

However, faced with all these unknown possibilities, an overwhelmed wine drinker can easily be panicked into playing it safe and choosing something tried and tested, thus missing out on sampling some of these diverse delights. There's arguably now more need for vinous guidance than ever before, which is what this book aims to provide. Supplying the tools for a smooth and satisfying journey, it will assist you to discover what you like, inspire you to seek it out, and ideally, along the way, give you the confidence to venture into uncharted territory, trying loads of great wines in the process!

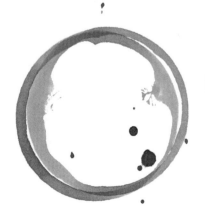

Taste!
Taste! Taste!

Okay, it's time to get active. If you're reading this book, it suggests that you've worked up a thirst for more knowledge — and for most of us who find ourselves intrigued by wine, this comes about when we stop drinking wine . . . and actually start tasting it. It's this difference between a passive and an active approach that's key to wine appreciation.

Luckily there's plenty of information to be soaked up from various sources to help you on your way. There's this book, and wine courses which can also offer great learning opportunities through a more comprehensive and orderly overview of wine. Then there are the likes of wine columns, magazines and internet sites that offer stimulating snapshots of a variety of wine-related topics and which can keep you abreast of the latest wine releases and news.

However, text is nothing without tasting, which is the main way you're going to learn about wine and get to know your palate and preferences. Each chapter of this book finishes with a selection of wines that exemplify its themes and which you can try for yourself. This practical element makes studying wine so much fun!

Getting to know your palate is a fascinating and sometimes

surprising affair. You may already have a good idea of what you like, but trying new wines can open doors to aromas, flavours and textures that you may have never experienced before and could convert you to types of wines you may have previously avoided.

As well as the recommendations in this book, do try and get as many new wines across your taste buds as you can manage. You don't have to develop a drinking habit or shell out countless dollars to do this, as there are many places where you can sip for next to nothing — and sometimes for free. These include wine shops that offer regular tastings instore, as well as larger tastings hosted by wineries who've grouped together to promote their region, and sometimes wine distributers. It's also good to get out to your local wine region — or venture further afield — and make the most of sampling wine at the cellar door, an activity that's often

BUFF OR BORE?

Most of us have probably encountered at least one of the species known as the lesser-spotted wine snob — thankfully 'lesser spotted' here, given New Zealand's egalitarian wine culture and lack of a gouty old guard intent on maintaining wine's mystique.

At worst, these snobs use their wine knowledge as a weapon to establish social superiority, delighting in frequent use of jargon and technical terms. Then there's the less offensive, but often equally tedious, type identified by their incessant twittering about what's in their glass. In doing so they fail to recognise that wine is just one component of life's rich blend.

Wine is an intriguing liquid, brimming with interesting associations that go way beyond what's in the glass or bottle. Those prepared to sniff out things a little further can take into consideration the following ingredients: a good-sized dose of geography, a liberal measure of the often-fascinating folk that make it, a drop each of history and culture and a slug of religion, politics and intrigue, and be rewarded with a recipe for conversation that's much more likely to be a source of entertainment than ennui.

accompanied by an informed commentary that can really help put the wines in context. You can also consider joining a club. From the North Shore to Gore, there are wine clubs all over the country, and joining them will offer opportunities to expand your tasting repertoire and imbibe with like-minded folk.

And next time you're buying a bottle for yourself, while there's nothing wrong with revisiting an old favourite, why not try a different wine. One that you've never drunk before. After you've finished this book, journeys into the unknown should lead you to exciting discoveries rather than the disappointing destinations that can result from a more random approach.

TASTE: how we do it

It seems staggering that it's still not entirely understood exactly how the human sense of smell — and consequently taste — works. While these senses are crucial in leading us to consume good things and avoid potentially harmful ones — as well as playing an important part in memory — we live in a visual culture that sees smell and taste largely underrated.

What we *do* know is that taste is detected by receptor cells clustered in the taste buds that are largely located on the tongue. These cells detect the five basic tastes: bitterness, sourness, saltiness, sweetness and the recently recognised savoury taste known as umami.

However, when it comes to sensing more sophisticated stimuli, the tongue is a pretty blunt instrument. It's actually the nose that does most of the work. This funnels the more subtle nuances

'Every wine enthusiast goes through a period of learning and reaches a point when they realise that they know more about the subject than many others. Most of us then experience a snobby phase before we see that it's a huge learning curve that will never end and that what we know is to be shared.'

Raymond Chan, *Regional Wines*

'Not only can wine really embody a sense of place, it can also bring to life the fruits of summers long gone. It's a slice of history.'

Mike Just, Clayridge, Marlborough

of what we're tasting up to olfactory receptor neurons situated within it, which feed this odiferous information to the olfactory bulb in the brain.

Each of us tastes things differently; for example, it's quite possible for your friend to find a particular wine as velvety as the voice of Whirimako Black, while to you it's as bitter and abrasive as Johnny Rotten, or perhaps you're the only one in a group to detect the aroma of banana in a wine's bouquet. Relax — you're not going bananas; it's most likely down to differences in genetic make-up. It's often touted that taste is a highly subjective area, and scientific studies give credence to this, suggesting that the perception of smells and tastes could be as unique to you as your fingerprint. Aromas of pears, sandalwood, some floral scents and bananas can go undetected by a significant proportion of people, while memory, expectations and experience also play their part in shaping our perceptions.

According to recent research, tasters can also be divided into three categories: 25% are non-tasters, 25% are super tasters and 50% are medium tasters. It comes down to the number of taste buds you have on your tongue. Super tasters are better endowed on this front, tasting things more vividly than most and are consequently more sensitive to flavours such as bitterness.

We may all be smelling and tasting slightly different things, but there's still enough common ground to make communicating about what various individuals find in a wine worthwhile. However, what's even more important is to create our own descriptions to build up a personal library of taste references through identifying the different components of a wine and noting their intensities.

FINDING THE WORDS

'When I find someone I respect writing about an edgy, nervous wine that dithered in the glass, I cringe,' observed writer and wine-lover Kingsley Amis in *Everyday Drinking*. 'You can call a wine red, and dry, and strong, and pleasant. After that, watch out . . .' I disagree with Amis, a *bon viveur*, who perhaps drank more wine than he tasted! While outpourings of purple prose can prove cloying, finding as many accurate descriptors for the smells, tastes and textures you're experiencing, then connecting them with different styles of wine, is what makes an expert taster. Super taster or not, using these powers of observation to make links are skills that can be developed, meaning we all start on a relatively level playing field.

When you've found the words you want to use, write them down. It's worth investing in a dedicated notebook for this purpose, not least because you'll then have a record to go back to when you need to refresh your memory. It's amazing how a wine can make an impression you think you'll never forget, but then become lost somewhere in the dusty cellars of the mind a few dozen wines later. Making a note about each wine you taste also helps to draw out more descriptors and helps to set them in your memory.

Learn the lingo

APPELLATION: a geographically designated quality wine district, often with official status and rules governing the wines produced there, which can range from entire regions to tiny areas. These include France's Appellation d'Origine Contrôlée (AOC), Italy's Denominazione di Origine Controllata (DOC) and Spain's Denomenación de Origen (DO). This information often appears on wine labels.

ASSEMBLAGE: the art of blending a wine using different components from different barrels, to vats, vineyards or even regions.

BARRIQUE: the French name for the 225-litre wooden barrel widely used in winemaking.

BIN: a collection of stored wine bottles stacked on top of each other, with a 'bin end' indicating remaining bottles left from a larger quantity and sold at a reduced price.

CHÂTEAU: this word literally translates to castle in French, but usually refers to a wine estate, regardless of whether a grand building is involved — as is the case with many wine estates in Bordeaux.

CLARET: the British name for red wine from Bordeaux.

CLASSICO: the Italian term for the historical centre of a region, theoretically with the area's best winegrowing conditions.

CLEANSKIN: a wine sold without a label; often used to anonymously shift volumes of surplus wine at a cheap price.

EN PRIMEUR: a practice in which a wine is sold on the futures market before it's bottled. It sounds like a bit of a gamble, but it's how many of the top wines of Bordeaux are sold.

ESTATE: usually indicates that a wine has been made from the winery's own vineyards and not from grapes that have been bought in.

EXTRACT: the dissolved solid material that provides intensity in a wine. Over-extraction is a criticism levelled at a wine in which techniques have been employed to maximise this characteristic at the expense of a wine's finesse.

FINESSE: a positive attribute in a wine that suggests delicacy and balance.

LEES: the combination of dead yeast cells, bits of grape skin and other insoluble materials that settle at the bottom of a barrel or vat, and which add complexity and texture to a wine (*sur lie* in French). Its effects can be maximised by stirring them up from time to time (a process called *bâtonnage*).

MAGNUM: a 1.5-litre wine bottle (equivalent to two standard wine bottles). The next size up is the three-litre jeroboam, and the largest is the mighty 30-litre melchizedek, which you'd practically need a crane to lift!

MASTER OF WINE: judged on theory and blind tasting, this rigorously tested wine qualification has a notoriously high failure rate, with fewer than 300 people worldwide able to put the coveted letters MW after their name (just eight of them here in New Zealand).

MUST: crushed grapes and their juice before they've been fermented.

NEW WORLD: the winemaking nations outside the world's traditional wine regions, the majority of which are situated in the Southern Hemisphere.

NOSE: the smell of a wine, also known as aroma or bouquet.

OLD WORLD: the traditional winemaking regions of Europe and the Mediterranean basin.

PALATE: the word regularly used to describe the taste and feel of a wine in the mouth.

TERROIR: a quintessentially French term used to evoke the favourable combination of site, climate and grape variety.

TYPICITY: from the French term *tipicité* and Italian *tipicità*, most often used to describe how a wine reflects the place in which it's grown (or terroir).

VARIETAL: a wine named after the single grape variety from which it has been made.

VIGNERON: the French term for winegrower.

STYLE TREKKING: what we taste

In *Star Trek*, the Vulcans follow a philosophy of Infinite Diversity in Infinite Combinations that regards progress and great things as flowing from the fusion of multiple elements. While it's debatable whether Spock and Co's culture permitted them to partake of a tipple, it's a concept that relates well to wine, the product of a diverse range of factors that result in an almost infinite combination of tastes and textures.

So let us now go where many tasters have gone before, and track the key components that make up wine.

Fruity

An unmistakeable fruity character is often one of the first things to leap out of you in a glass of wine. Ironically, it's only wines made from the Muscat grape that actually taste grapey, while most other wines conjure up flavours from a wide spectrum of fruits — from citrus, through berry and stone fruits, to more tropical specimens. Wines made in warmer climates and in certain styles can also exhibit fruit characters that are more cooked or dried, such as raisins, dried figs, prunes or jammy notes.

Modern winemaking tends to accentuate fruit, which is a major stylistic trait in many wines from the New World (see page 18). However, in Old World countries, such as France and Italy, there is often more emphasis on texture, with fruit a less obvious element.

Sweet and dry

Sweetness at varying levels, and also dryness, are other components registered early and are mainly sensed on the tip of the tongue. Given these are something we're used to encountering on a regular basis these tastes are relatively easy to spot. However, it's worth bearing in mind that ripe fruit can give an impression of sweetness, as can alcohol, while acidity can make a sweet wine appear far drier than its actual sugar levels would suggest.

Savoury

Umami, meaning savoury in Japanese, has only recently become recognised as the fifth primary taste. It's a flavour imparted by glutamate, a type of amino acid that subtly expands and rounds flavours. It occurs naturally in foods, with particularly high levels found in cheeses such as Parmesan, as well as in mushrooms, 'meatier' fish, many beans and in wines, especially riper, full-bodied reds and whites that have spent a long time maturing their yeast cells.

Herbs and spice

Wines can also conjure up different herbs and spices. Herbal notes can come from a wine's grape variety or under-ripe flavours, while spicy notes are sometimes a characteristic of certain grape varieties or can be derived from contact with oak.

Creamy

Rich, creamy or buttery characters are often found in barrel-fermented whites that have undergone malolactic fermentation, which converts a grape's sharp-tasting malic acid to the softer lactic acid (see page 106).

Minerally

Some of the greatest wines are said to exhibit a character akin to stones, described as minerally. As few of us are in the habit of pebble-sucking, this mineral taste is harder to get your head round than the fruit flavours we're more familiar with. However, it can be likened to the mineral salts found in sparkling water, the aroma that comes off wet stones or the smell created through rubbing two flints together.

Nutty

Most often found in white or wood-aged examples, there are many different kinds of nutty notes that can be found in wine. These include the likes of almonds, hazelnuts, walnuts and pecans.

Animal

While an unappealing bouquet of barnyard can be due to a wine

fault, many wines exhibit attractive 'animally' notes, from a whiff of well-hung game (evoked in the expression gamey), to grilled meat or leather.

Earthy/forest floor

Mature red wines in particular often conjure up nuances of decaying leaves, truffles, mushrooms and generally earthy notes. This may sound a bit rotten, but it is to be found in some of the best red wines.

Smoke/toast

These flavours, which range from smoky bacon to buttered toast, tend to come from wine that's been in contact with oak.

TALKING TEXTURE

You don't just taste wine, you feel it, too. Like skin, the tongue and mouth contain numerous nerve endings that can sense the feel (texture) of a wine. This texture can be likened to a wine's skeleton, upon which the flesh of its flavours are hung.

It's the textural elements of a wine that can make a sip such a dynamic experience as it travels across your palate, provoking sensations of silkiness to astringency, lightness to weight. Some wines, such as Sauvignon Blanc, will ricochet across your mouth in a riot of acid. Others, like Pinot Noir, unfurl themselves slowly with a satin-like sensuousness.

Crisp

The feeling of crispness in a wine is due to higher levels of acidity, something that straddles taste and texture. It's readily recognised in wines from cool climates such as New Zealand where it provides a zingy hit that makes wines with higher acid levels so refreshing to drink, and easy to describe with words such as 'crisp', 'fresh' and 'zesty'.

Acidity is what makes your mouth water. Relatively elevated acid levels form an important part of a wine's structure and set it apart from drinks such as beer and spirits. While the term may conjure up something tart or sour, in the absence of acidity wine would lose its attractive fresh lift and feel rather flat.

Chewy

Wines containing a lot of tannins are described as being chewy. Found predominantly in red wine — and imparted by a grape's skin and pips, as well as contact with oak — tannins produce a drying sensation in the mouth. In abundance their astringency can feel rather tough, but not only do they give structure to a wine, they also help a wine to age and will often soften with time. For a taste of tannins outside wine, brew up a strong cuppa, as tea also contains considerable amounts.

Alcoholic

Fermentation produces ethyl alcohol (ethanol), which does a lot more than just get you merry. Most importantly, it carries the wine's flavours and has a viscosity that contributes to its body and perceptions of sweetness. Usually at levels between 7–15%, it's not

FADS AND FASHIONS

Wine drinkers can be a fickle bunch and many trends come and go. It doesn't seem that long ago when Kiwis were knocking back Müller-Thurgau. When it became passé, we couldn't get enough Chardonnay. Then Sauvignon Blanc came on the scene, becoming New Zealand's most widely consumed wine a few years back and, like the little black dress, has swiftly acquired classic status likely to ensure its popularity for years to come. That's unless our thirst for Pinot Gris continues at current rates or if a lesser-known variety such as Viognier becomes a mainstream hit.

Our taste in reds has increasingly moved away from the Aussie staples of the past to our own Pinot Noir. There's also a small underground following emerging for homegrown Syrah, while Spanish reds are hot stuff.

that easy to pick up unless it's particularly high; it can produce a warming or even burning sensation in the mouth and throat, described as 'hot'.

Full- or light-bodied

Body, also known as mouth feel, is the perception of weight a wine has in the mouth. Light-bodied wines tend to hail from cooler climates or are characteristic of certain grape varieties, and can be just as intense in flavour as heavier wines. Full-bodied wines tend to be more concentrated, with higher levels of extract and alcohol.

TASTING TECHNIQUES

There's more to tasting wine than taking a quick slurp and then swallowing. Slowing down the procedure, taking the time to think about what you're tasting and applying a few simple techniques will enable you to make the most of your mouthful.

Before you start, I recommend that you get yourself a good tasting glass such as the standard XL5, which can be bought from many specialist wine stores. Pour just a small sample of wine into it so you can give the wine a good swirl without drenching yourself or anyone in your immediate vicinity!

Squizz: looking at wine

The appearance of a wine can tell you quite a lot about its personality before you've even allowed it to pass your lips. In the first instance you're looking at colour and clarity. Colour and its intensity varies between grape varieties and wine styles, which —

just like people — start to look different with age. Red wines become paler and more russet in colour as they get older, while whites become darker and more golden. However, even quite a young wine that's been in contact with oak may display a golden tint.

Murkiness in wine is often a bad sign, suggesting a rogue re-fermentation in the bottle or bacterial issues, but cloudiness in some red wines could simply be caused by the stirring up of sediment. Generally speaking, though, most healthy wines should be clear and bright.

While bubbles are obviously present in sparkling wine, they may also appear in still wines, often due to winemakers leaving in a bit of CO_2 in lighter whites for added freshness. However, bubbles in still wine, accompanied by yeasty aromas are bad news, again suggesting an unwanted secondary fermentation.

You may have come across references to a wine's legs; to spot them, simply swirl the glass and look for traces that run down the inside of the glass. Also known as tears, their presence indicates either high-alcohol or sugar levels in a wine.

> 'Good wine is made from a mixture of bees, butterflies, good fortune and enthusiasm.'
>
> James Millton, Millton Vineyard, Gisborne

Swirl and sniff: assessing aromas

Swirling the glass helps to release a wine's all-important aromas. A good swirl can be mastered by moving your glass in circles on a flat surface before trying the same movement in the air. Take a good few sniffs and try to describe what you smell. If you're having trouble finding the words, look at the terms connected with the various styles and see if any fit what you're experiencing.

Even when you're not sniffing out the aromas in wine, try to pay more attention to identifying the smells around you; doing this on a regular basis helps hone the sense of smell. (And if your wine's bouquet smells less than rosy, see page 111 for more information on identifying common wine faults.)

Slurp: a good mouthful

When taking your first sip of a wine, take a medium-sized mouthful. Swish it around your mouth so it reaches all of your taste buds and becomes aerated to release those all-important molecules that will work wonders on your nose.

You may have heard raucous slurping sounds made by professional tasters; they do this to let air in through their mouth and pass it across the wine to get as many aromas as possible up into that olfactory bulb. You can give this a go yourself, but it's in no way obligatory. Just be sure to note the different elements you're experiencing from that mouthful.

Size up: judging quality

After holding the wine in your mouth long enough to note its key characters (see Taste Tick List earlier on page 19) you can either swallow the wine or spit it out if you don't want to feel the effects of the alcohol or prefer to keep a clear head in the face of more wines to try. But your observations shouldn't stop here — just as the flavours of a great wine won't. When tasting really good wines, these flavours can linger positively for some time after you've swallowed, while in the simpler and usually cheaper wines they'll disappear quite quickly. This aftertaste is called a wine's 'length' or 'finish', and often offers an idea of a wine's quality.

So what makes a good wine? Given the subjective nature of people's tastes highlighted by the heated debates at many wine tastings and competitions, opinion can vary when it comes to the finer judgements on a wine. However, whatever one's personal preference, an almost universal criterion that forms the basis of many professional assessments centres on complexity and balance.

Think back to the wine you've just tasted. If you've come up with lots of positive descriptors it's likely to be a relatively complex wine, especially if it's one where every sip reveals something more. But if you've only managed to find a few adjectives to describe it, it's probably something quite simple.

Balance is the other hallmark of a good wine. All the elements should be in harmony with one another. And unless it's a young red wine where tannins can be quite overt before slipping back with age, nothing should stick out, such as searing acidity, gum-numbing tannins or a cloying sweetness that's not supported by cleansing acidity.

GET TASTING

Theory is nothing without practice. Why not get some friends together and try the following six wines that will illustrate some of the key components explored in this chapter. Included are some guidelines for the wines to try, with options at different price levels. You may well be able to get less expensive examples but unless these are on special, they may not make the points as clearly.

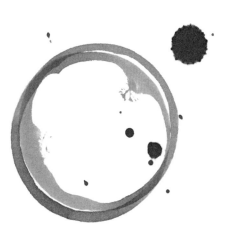

Make friends with your local wine merchant (see Recommended Retailers on page 240) and they'll be able to assist you with your selections.

1

CRISP SWEET WHITE

Look for a Riesling from a cool climate with an alcohol level of 12% or below; the lower the alcohol, the sweeter the wine is likely to be.

SUGGESTED WINES

Sherwood Stratum Waipara Riesling, $15–20

Dr Loosen 'Dr L' Mosel Riesling, Germany, $20–25

Pegasus Bay Waipara Riesling, $25–30

TASTING NOTE: As well as taking on board the light aromatics of blossom, peach and citrus, notice how the wine feels quite sweet at first but finishes on a far drier note than you'd initially expect, demonstrating the balance between sweetness and acidity. The body is also relatively light, although the flavours are quite intense.

2

RICH AND AROMATIC WHITE

The Gewürztraminer grape makes some of the most highly aromatic wines, with good examples hailing from our shores and France's Alsace region.

SUGGESTED WINES

Waimea Nelson Gewürztraminer, $20–25

Johanneshof Marlborough Gewürztraminer, $25–30

Vinoptima Gisborne Gewürztraminer, $30+

TASTING NOTE: Get your nose around those exotically spicy aromas, as well as the variety's classic notes of rose petal and lychee. Rich and intense, Gewürztraminer can be quite oily in texture and has relatively low acidity, which will make it feel far softer and fatter in the mouth than a Riesling.

3 MINERALLY WHITE

Some varieties, regions or styles of winemaking produce wines with this prized character, which is regularly accompanied by fresh acidity. Mineral notes are most notable in cool climate Chardonnays from regions such as Chablis, many Rieslings and Spain's Albariño grape.

SUGGESTED WINES

Kumeu River Village Kumeu Chardonnay, $15–20

Cave Lugny Macon Lugny 'Les Charmes', Burgundy, France, $20–25

A Chablis, such as Pascal Bouchard Chablis, France, $25–35

TASTING NOTE: You should be able to get a whiff of wet stones and citrus on the nose as well as a definite minerally note on the palate, where it's fused with fresh mouth-watering citrus and sometimes quite steely acidity.

4

FRESH LIGHT RED

A grape like Gamay that makes France's Beaujolais is the ultimate light and fruity red.

SUGGESTED WINES

Te Mata Woodthorpe Hawkes Bay Gamay Noir, $15–20
Château du Bourg Beaujolais Villages, France, $20–25
Georges Duboeuf Beaujolais Saint-Amour, France, $25–30

TASTING NOTE: Lots of bright berry fruit such as raspberry, strawberry and red cherry, flowers and perhaps even a bubblegum-like note from a winemaking technique called maceration carbonique often employed in making Beaujolais. The wine is light in weight, soft in texture with almost imperceptible tannins, and a fruit character that's to the fore.

5 BIG FRUITY RED

Warmer climates and grapes such as Shiraz and Cabernet produce wines with bags of body and alcohol, making Aussie Shirazes and Shiraz Cabernet blends perfect examples of this style.

SUGGESTED WINES

Wyndham Estate Bin 555 South East Australia Shiraz, Australia, $15–17

Taylors Eighty Acres Clare Valley Cabernet Shiraz Merlot, Australia, $17–20

Heartland Shiraz, Australia, $20–25

TASTING NOTE: In a warm-climate wine acidity is lower, the fruit is ripe and sweet tasting — although there may not actually be much sugar in the wine — and concentrated. Oak is often used on these big ripe styles, imparting spicy cedary notes, and there could be a hint of that elusive umami (see page 20).

6 CHEWY RED

For wines with the greatest tannic grip, look to European reds, especially French ones that include a fair bit of Cabernet Sauvignon, such as blends from Bordeaux.

SUGGESTED WINES

Finca Sobreno, Toro, Spain, $15–20

Château Carbonneau Cuvée Fût de Chêne, Sainte Foy de
   Bordeaux, France, $20–25

Château de Lugagnac Bordeaux Superieur, France, $25–30

TASTING NOTE: Tannins provide the backbone to this wine; feel how these dry the mouth and slightly numb the gums. It's also worth comparing the oaky notes between this and the big fruity red as in these Old World examples: older French oak barrels are likely to have been used which tend to leave a more understated spicy note.

CHAPTER TWO

Great Whites

'There are thousands of grape varieties in the world: be vinous promiscuous!'

Nicola Belsham, Wineseeker, Wellington

From the seductive spice of Gewürztraminer to the pungent herbs of Sauvignon Blanc, much of a wine's character comes from the grape variety from which it's made. While region and winemaking also leave their mark, get to grips with your grapes and you're well on your way to making an educated guess at what you might find in the bottle, especially as most wines from the Southern Hemisphere have their grape variety emblazoned boldly across their labels.

There are more than 10,000 grape varieties in the world today, each capable of imbuing a wine with its individual personality. Yet most of these remain below the radar of even the most knowledgeable wine buff.

The so-called classic or noble grapes are the ones with which we're most familiar. Also known as international varieties, while most originally hail from France, they've gained a status and popularity from being grown sucessfully around the globe. Many people tend to stick to a small selection of these tried and tested varieties, but it's worth moving out of that comfort zone to sample something else. As changes in grape growing and winemaking practices mean styles are always evolving it's worth checking out a variety you've not tried in a while; different countries and regions have their own distinctive expressions of the same grapes and there are rich pickings to be found among lesser known varieties, which can open up new and fascinating dimensions of flavour.

While the traditional winegrowing countries have had many centuries to work out what grows best where, newer wine nations such as New Zealand are still matching grape to place. Some classic combinations have already been struck, for example,

Sauvignon Blanc in Marlborough, while others are yet to be discovered as new varieties start to enter our grape-growing mix.

Leading whites

SAUVIGNON BLANC: herbal highs
(So-VEEN-yon Blonk)

Cat's pee on a gooseberry bush or bungy-jumping naked through one are just some of the colourful descriptions that have been used to conjure up the vibrant and visceral experience provided by a sip of New Zealand Sauvignon Blanc. This variety's zesty and herbaceous nature, which makes it one of the easiest varieties to recognise, has thrilled wine drinkers the world over in its variations — from New Zealand to northern France.

Sauvignon Blanc is an ancient grapevine likely to have originated in France's Loire Valley, where some of the world's most highly regarded Sauvignons are made. These include Sancerre and Pouilly Fumé, which are more restrained than our New Zealand versions, with distinctive flinty and minerally notes. The Sauvignon variety also forms part of the blend in white Bordeaux, which can be elegant and lightly oaked with added weight and longevity provided by its partner Sémillon.

As a growing number of countries around the world try their hand at Sauvignon, internationally it has attained status as one of the most popular white varieties. The best examples come from

'Good Sauvignon Blanc has that burst of flavour combined with real texture and a taste of place. At the end of a day in the winery, it is usually the first glass we drink while relaxing in the cellar door, and then late at night we often return to it for its freshness and vibrancy.'

Brian Bicknell, Mahi, Marlborough

the cooler climates that allow the full expression of its aromatic intensity. These include minerally and dried herb expressions from Austria, a light and racy style from northern Italy, soft fresh specimens from coastal Chile and riper more tropical Sauvignons from the cooler parts of South Africa.

However, it's here in New Zealand, or Marlborough more specifically, where winemakers have produced a unique style that's captivated palates across the world. Described as Sauvignon on steroids, our version of this wine is particularly pungent, combining fresh herbs with ripe notes of passionfruit and gooseberry backed by a zingy citrus acidity. It's these high levels of passionfruit flavours, caused by compounds called volatile thiols, that research has found both to be far higher in Marlborough Sauvignons and particularly preferred by its drinkers.

With fruit and aromatics so much to the fore in most Sauvignons, using oak that can mask these is relatively rare. When wooden barrels *are* used, which happens more in France and to New Zealand's top Sauvignons, they tend to be older barrels that add to a wine's texture without imparting much flavour of their own.

Sauvignon's wines tend to live fast and die young. While some French examples are able to age for up to a decade, unlike most other noble varieties, Sauvignon Blanc wines are not known for their longevity. They're often best enjoyed within a couple of years of their vintage, as it's when they're young and fresh that most Sauvignons excel.

Swirl, sniff and slurp

Green herbs, cat's pee, cut grass, gooseberry, passionfruit, asparagus, jalapeño, flint, mineral, blackcurrant leaf, melon, apple, lemon, lime, blackcurrant, crisp

CHARDONNAY: comeback queen
(SHAR-don-ay)

Chameleon-like Chardonnay is the David Bowie of the grape world: it's arguably got little intrinsic identity of its own, absorbs its influences like a sponge, but still makes great stuff. In recent decades it has also regularly reinvented itself; from the big oaky buttery brutes of yore to the fruitier, more refined examples in evidence today.

Given its somewhat nebulous personality, the techniques a winemaker chooses to apply to Chardonnay can leave a significant stamp on the finished wine. One of the key ways they can influence the style is deciding whether or not to 'oak' the wine. Chardonnay has a great affinity with wood, which when well employed can enhance its character through adding nutty, toasty notes and giving it greater weight. However, there has been a tendency in New World wine countries to use it far too heavy-handedly, so that the tasting experience can be more reminiscent of sucking on a plank than savouring the variety's subtle charms.

Thankfully, this style — in which vanilla or coconutty oak was often joined by overblown buttery notes — is no longer widespread, but has left many people with the conviction that Chardonnay is not to their taste. Contemporary Chardonnays tend to have much less oak, and in some cases no wood at all, with these labelled unoaked or unwooded.

'Chardonnay — so layered, complex and inviting, at once revealing its site origins in fruit complexity and flavour profile along with the subtle hand of the winemaker.'

Tony Bish, Sacred Hill,
Hawke's Bay

In their pure unadulterated form, Chardonnays from cool climates such as New Zealand's South Island and France's Chablis (in the north of the Burgundy region) are often crisp and lighter-bodied, with fruit in the spectrum of apple, melon and white peach, sometimes joined by the minerally character so celebrated in great white wines.

In warmer climates, such as much of Australia and a warmer New Zealand region like Gisborne, Chardonnays tend to be softer and fuller bodied, with more tropical fruit characters such as pineapple and fruit salad.

Chardonnay's heartland is France's Burgundy where some of the greatest examples are made. However, as it's easy to grow almost anywhere, over the years it has popped up in most of the winegrowing regions of the world.

Its ubiquitous nature and the sea of humdrum homogenised examples churned out at the cheaper end of the market during the 1990s gave rise to the ABC brigade, those who demanded Anything But Chardonnay. However, grown with care and treated sensitively in the winery, this noble variety can be coaxed into producing genuinely enthralling and truly diverse wines that can be numbered among some of the greatest and longest-lived white wines of the world.

Swirl, sniff and slurp

Stone fruit, melon, fruit salad, citrus, toasty, nutty, mocha, butter, cream, vanilla, mineral, crisp, rich

RIESLING: a fresh paradox
(REE-zling)

Riesling has to be one of the most paradoxical of grape varieties. It manages to be both light and intense, cerebral and sensual, balancing sweetness with acidity, and while loved by winemakers and wine writers, is often spurned by the wider drinking public.

It's a grape that's able to express the place in which it is grown arguably like no other white variety, at the same time preserving its distinct identity. This is reflected in the intriguing diversity of its different expressions that run across an exhilarating spectrum of citrus, stone fruit, flowers and minerals.

There's a Riesling for every occasion to suit an impressive range of foods and tastes: from the limey bone-dry examples from Australia's Clare Valley, to the richer styles of France's Alsace, through to the sweeter low-alcohol German versions and luscious late harvest and noble wines, plus 'a bit of everything' in New Zealand (although off dry is the most widely made style here).

Unfortunately, it's a variety that comes with an undeserved stigma — no thanks to the cheap and not so cheerful insipid semi-sweet German examples seen here in the 1960s and 1970s, along with the local Riesling rip-offs of that era which were more often mongrel Müller-Thurgau-based wines than pure-bred Riesling.

Another seemingly contradictory characteristic embodied by Riesling is the way that its inherently crisp acidity makes wines with considerable sweetness actually taste quite dry. This has caused difficulties when their makers attempt to describe the various styles, an issue that the International Riesling Foundation hopes to address through the introduction of a new taste scale

'When made with traditional methods, Riesling has the ability to really show where it has been grown, which is in a wide range of suitable soils and climates, where the grape is capable of producing the most elegant and exciting wines.'

Matt Donaldson,
Pegasus Bay, Waipara

that wineries can feature on their labels. Running from dry to sweet, the scale cleverly takes into consideration the interplay between the sweetness and acidity of each wine.

Good Riesling has an amazing ability to age. In time it can transform from something floral and fruity to a wine that's honeyed, toasty, or displaying what's described as a kerosene note, while retaining its core freshness.

Riesling is the only so-called classic variety not to come from France. Originating in Germany (the source, along with Alsace, of its benchmark examples), the best Rieslings come from cooler vineyards, which have the longer growing seasons the grapes require to ripen slowly and build up the intense flavours that create the excitement of its best examples.

Despite the efforts of its makers and the massive amount of column centimetres devoted to it by Riesling-mad wine critics, its final paradox is why a variety that's behind some of the greatest wines in the world remains so woefully underrated.

Swirl, sniff and slurp

Granite, slate, mineral, blossom, floral, peach, lemon, lime, apple, grapefruit, honey, toasty, kerosene, crisp, intense

Up-and-coming aromatics

PINOT GRIS: rising star
(PEE-noh GREE)

Variety is certainly the spice of life when it comes to Pinot Gris. Made in a multitude of styles, examples span the simple and fruit-driven to intense and complex, lean and mineral to fat and spicy, steel fermented to barrel-aged . . . and everything in between.

Pinot Gris has always been a staple in Alsace, reaching its zenith in the region's rich and spicy expressions. It's also an important grape in northern Italy, where it makes a fresher earlier picked and often quite neutral style marketed under its other well-known moniker, Pinot Grigio.

A growing global thirst for this variety has prompted a proliferation in plantings, especially on local soils where, in under a decade, Pinot Gris has emerged from near obscurity to become New Zealand's fourth most widely cultivated grape.

While unlikely to scale the racy heights reached by nobler whites such as Riesling and Chardonnay, well-made Pinot Gris can be wonderfully beguiling. It often displays a gentle acidity, mouth-filling quince and pear fruit and a subtle seasoning of spice that has seduced many a Chardonnay fan with its comparable crowd-pleasing character.

However, producers who've been Pinot Greedy — or just plain Pinot Green and allowed the vine to produce the vast quantities of grapes that it's wont to do if left unchecked — have made some less than inspirational examples. Over-cropped Pinot Gris can be crushingly dull, as seen in many examples from New Zealand's first wave of Gris.

Thankfully, as growers come to understand the need to curb its exuberant personality in the vineyard, more characterful and intensely flavoured wines are making it into the bottle. It's simply not possible to make decent Pinot Gris at similar crop levels to Sauvignon, which is why it's more expensive. It pays to beware of low-price Gris, as there's a good chance it will be boring and bland.

Just as quality is becoming more consistent, styles have started to settle down among our homegrown examples, which in the past included some dramatic stylistic swings between vintages even from individual producers as they experimented with this new grape on the block.

Most have now migrated to a gently off-dry style, although many labels are still not explicit as to what you can expect. Many winemakers, for example, appear to be shy about the issue of sweetness, and tend to avoid mentioning this on the label, while those making dry examples are much more upfront.

The good news is that buying Pinot Gris today is certainly far less of a minefield than it used to be. The quality is generally much better as experience and competition have increased in tandem, while today's increasingly savvy drinkers are far less tolerant of grey Gris and pressure builds for it to be great.

Swirl, sniff and slurp

Pear, quince, cinnamon, nutmeg, pepper, oily, soft

GEWÜRZTRAMINER: old spice
(ger-VURTZ-tramin-er)

When conjuring up the characters of Gewürztraminer, the description can make it sound more like a perfume than a wine. This is one ultra-aromatic variety, infused with notes of exotic spice, rose water, blossom, citrus peel and lychee that can almost tempt you to dab a drop or two behind your ears as well as drink it!

Würtz means spice in German, while traminer comes from the Tyrolean town of Tramin in Italy, where the grape may well have originated.

Featuring pinkish-coloured berries, the Gewürztraminer vine produces quite deeply coloured wines, often rich and viscous with lower acidity and higher alcohol levels. While it does well in a wider variety of locations than fellow aromatics Riesling and Sauvignon Blanc, it still benefits from cooler climates that help it retain its keynote fragrance.

In the northeastern French wine region of Alsace, it's considered a noble variety, where its incarnations range from dry to sweet and are rated among the finest in the world. Gewürztraminer is also made in Germany, Italy and Austria, as well as in many of the newer winegrowing countries of the world.

It is grown in small quantities throughout New Zealand, where the best examples combine the grape's powerful

NEW GRAPES IN NEW ZEALAND

The varieties found in New Zealand vineyards today are far different to what was there in the late 1980s. Gone are the humdrum hybrids and mundane Müller-Thurgau, which have been almost entirely replaced by higher quality varieties, especially the aromatic whites that suit our cooler climate so well. The top five varieties — Sauvignon Blanc, Pinot Noir, Chardonnay, Pinot Gris and Merlot — currently make up over three-quarters of the country's wine production. However, greater diversity is being injected into our vineyards through the increased availability of a wider range of grapes. Some of these, such as the Austrian grape Grüner Veltliner or Spanish variety Albariño, have never before been planted in New Zealand, opening up the possibility of some exciting new combinations.

Could there be more magnificent 'marriages' in the offing, such as those between Marlborough and Sauvignon or Central Otago and Pinot Noir? Time will tell.

aromatic intensity with the freshness it can lack when grown in warmer locations.

Despite being very well suited to the country's conditions, it remains a minority grape here, which may have more to do with the difficulty in pronouncing its multi-syllabic Germanic name rather than its taste or quality!

Swirl, sniff and slurp

Rose petals, rose water, Turkish delight, exotic, spice, lychee, ginger, quinine, soft, oily

VIOGNIER: exotic and quixotic
(vee-ON-yay)

Exotic and erratic, opulent and once incredibly rare, Viognier's quixotic character almost resulted in it becoming extinct. But it is now back from the brink, with New Zealand and Australia among the few countries spearheading its recent renaissance.

Viognier is an aromatic variety making distinctive full-bodied wines that can best be described as fusing the floral freshness of Riesling and the spice of Gewürztraminer with the weight of a Chardonnay. Often very perfumed, Viognier can also possess an intriguing salty, savoury umami-like flavour and a grip and intensity that has seen it regarded as a red-wine drinker's white. It's always relatively high in alcohol, which along with its viscous texture and the grape's naturally low acidity can give an impression of sweetness when in fact most wines made from this grape are dry.

Viognier is notoriously capricious to grow and it often bears very little fruit. Growers must also wait for the grapes to become ultra-ripe before picking, which only allows a very small window in which to harvest them in their full fragrant glory.

It was probably its capricious nature that resulted in it falling out of favour in France, with just 14 hectares of the variety remaining by 1968. But in the 1990s a gradual revival, spurred by interest in Rhône varieties in California, started winegrowers planting it again in France. Before long it was also being planted in Australia, Chile and now New Zealand, where interest in the examples from warmer regions, such as Hawke's Bay and Gisborne, is starting to become as intense as the wine's flavours.

Swirl, sniff and slurp

Apricot, peach, spice, musk, honeysuckle, oily, soft

Lesser-known nobility

SÉMILLON: delicious but endangered
(sem-EE-on)

It seems Sémillon might be heading the way of the kiwi, blue whale and giant panda — soon to be added to the endangered species list. Underrated and currently unfashionable, this potentially gorgeous grape is being foresaken by winegrowers in New Zealand and worldwide in favour of trendier varieties.

Like the wine from many other grapes, which have been planted in the wrong places and handled unsympathetically, Sémillon can lack excitement. However, its many scintillating expressions more than justify its noble ranking.

It's an incredibly versatile grape. In its heartland of Bordeaux, Sémillon is blended with Sauvignon Blanc to add weight to the region's dry wines. Its susceptibility to botrytis — the 'noble rot' that concentrates a grape's sugars and flavours — also makes it a key component of Sauternes, Bordeaux's great dessert wine, as well as other stickies around the world.

As a stand-alone variety it can be made in a rich barrel-fermented style or left fresh and citrusy. It also ages well, witnessed in the unique early-picked low-alcohol examples of

Australia's Hunter Valley, which metamorphose from something light, tight and lemony in their youth to rich, honeyed and toasty wines with time.

Once allegedly the most-planted grape in the world, Sémillon has fallen out of favour in recent years. Even in Bordeaux, the grape's most important region, interest in it is dwindling. And we're seeing less and less Sémillon here, too, both as imports or from our own vineyards. Sadly, only a handful of our winemakers now make straight Sémillon, or Sémillon Sauvignon blends, which is doubly depressing as most of these are wonderful wines that highlight the potential of the variety when planted in suitable sites.

Swirl, sniff and slurp

Lemon, lime, lanolin, butter, toast, honey, peach

CHENIN BLANC: Loire lovely
(shen-AN blonk)

Like Sémillon, Chenin Blanc is another noble variety that remains woefully unappreciated and relatively unknown in this country. Little remains in our vineyards, with very few producers making straight examples, despite our cool climate's suitability to producing interesting wines from this variety.

In France's Loire Valley, Chenin Blanc makes some of the region's top wines, which include the minerally bone-dry Savennières and the Vouvrays which range in style from dry to very sweet and sparkling.

Outside the Loire, South Africa and California are the only

other countries to embrace the variety with enthusiasm. While it is able to retain its acidity in warmer climates, the bulk of examples made in these countries have tended to be fresh if fairly neutral wines.

Known in South Africa as Steen, Chenin Blanc is the county's most widely planted grape. While the majority of it is made in a simple fruity style, producers focused on making more expressive examples are crafting Chenins with the understated power and mineral characters that make the grape great.

Chenin Blanc can be something of an acquired taste, but it's the variety's distinctive characteristics that endear it to its fans. At its heart is its crisp acidity, which can also be accompanied by honeyed notes, even in dry wines, and more outré notes of wet wool and hay. The best Chenins have immense concentration and can age for years.

Swirl, sniff and slurp

Honeysuckle, wax, almond, lanolin, citrus, melon, nut, apple, quince, honey, musk, marzipan, wet wool, hay

Other whites

There are many more white varieties worth trying. These include Muscat, an aromatic and full-flavoured variety of international repute, with a grapey, musky and spicy character. It's responsible for the sweet sparkling wines from Asti, the fine dry and sweeter late harvest examples from Alsace, as well as Australia's luscious fortified liqueur Muscats.

Also watch out for Italy's Arneis (ah-NACE); this 'little rascal' (the literal translation of its name) is just coming onstream in our vineyards where it's resulting in fresh, full-bodied and frequently quite high-alcohol wines with notes of stone fruit, pear and nut.

Another exciting variety hitting the country — in imported form from its homeland of Austria, and in tiny quantities now from New Zealand — is Grüner Veltliner (GROO-ner FELT-lee-ner). An intense minerally wine with a distinctive white pepper note, it's become increasingly trendy in the United States, where they've overcome their difficulty in pronouncing its name by shortening it to Gru-Vee, a moniker that kind of suits the classy wines made from this hip grape.

"There are more than 10,000 grape varieties in the world today, each capable of imbuing a wine with individual personality."

1 SAUVIGNON BLANC

SUGGESTED WINES

Redwood Pass Marlborough Sauvignon Blanc, $15–20

TerraVin Marlborough Sauvignon Blanc, $20–25

A Loire Sauvignon such as Henri Bourgeois Le Petit Bourgeois,
France, $25–30

TASTING NOTE: Herbal notes are the hallmarks of the variety
seen in these classic Sauvignons from Marlborough and the
Loire: from dried herbs to green or even likened to cat's pee
or sweat! Aromas should certainly be to the fore, supported
by zesty citrus acidity in a dry palate where an impression of
sweetness can come from its ripe fruit.

2 CHARDONNAY

SUGGESTED WINES

Morton Estate Hawkes Bay Chardonnay, $15–20

Hunter's Marlborough Chardonnay, $20–25

Ata Rangi Petrie Wairarapa Chardonnay, $25–30

TASTING NOTE: Sniffing and sipping a classic Chardonnay should conjure up stone fruit, often backed by a fresh citrus acidity and a touch of toastiness from the use of oak. Most good Chardonnays are made dry.

3 DRY RIESLING

SUGGESTED WINES

Riverby Estate Marlborough Riesling, $15–20
Fromm La Strada Marlborough Dry Riesling, $20–25
Framingham Marlborough Dry Riesling, $25–30

TASTING NOTE: Riesling's inherently high acidity is particularly noticeable in examples where no sugar has been left as a foil. The best combine delicate flavours of peach and sometimes blossom with an exhilarating citrus mineral core. If you're tasting an older vintage, such as the Framingham, these primary fruit aromas and flavours will be giving way to toasty honeyed notes, and often a distinctive kerosene-like quality.

4

PINOT GRIS

SUGGESTED WINES

Villa Maria Private Bin East Coast Pinot Gris, $15–20

Kaituna Valley The Summerhill Canterbury Vineyard Pinot
  Gris, $20–25

Neudorf Brightwater Nelson Pinot Gris, $25–30

TASTING NOTE: Wines made from the Pinot Gris grape vary in sweetness, but most will have a hint. There's often a liberal sprinkling of spice on the nose — from cinnamon and nutmeg to more peppery nuances — while pear and quince are the fruits most often associated with it. With lower acidity, it feels soft often with an oily texture in the mouth, and can even feel a little hot going down the throat due to its higher alcohol content.

5 VIOGNIER

SUGGESTED WINES

Yalumba Y Series Viognier, Autralia, $15–20

TW Estate Gisborne Viognier, $20–25

Trinity Hill Gimblett Gravels Viognier, $25–30

TASTING NOTE: It's hard not to linger over the nose on this one, with its apricot, musk and exotic spice. Another low acid and high-alcohol variety, Viognier can feel very weighty and oily in the mouth, with the best hiding their alcohol under the intense flavours of which the variety is capable.

6 CHENIN BLANC

SUGGESTED WINES

Forrest Marlborough Chenin Blanc, $20–24

Millton Te Arai Vineyard Gisborne Chenin Blanc, $25–30

Marc Bredif Vouvray, Loire, France, $25–30

TASTING NOTE: Chenin Blanc can have quite delicate honey and honeysuckle aromas, but very often packs a punch on the palate with zingy lemony acidity, mineral notes and the variety's intriguing characters of lanolin, wet wool and wax that are often accompanied by honeyed notes regardless of whether the wine's sweet or dry. The suggested examples are on the drier side.

CHAPTER THREE

Seeing Red

'A great grape variety is a vehicle with which man can elicit
the subtleties of expression inherent in a good site.'

Jeff Sinnott, Amisfield, Central Otago and Ostler, Waitaki Valley

An added dimension to red wines is the texture and colour due to the fact that unlike whites, red grapes are fermented with their skins. These provide tannins for structure and tinge the wines with colours, spanning light pinky reds and russets to purples and opaque inky hues.

The Big Reds

PINOT NOIR: passion and peacock's tails
(PEE-noh NWAR)

Pinot Noir has the power to ignite the passion of its admirers like almost no other variety. Making light-bodied wines, it can be overlooked by those who mistakenly equate quality with power. But for those seduced by its often ethereal charms, there is no greater grape.

Pinot Noir is something of a subtle and restrained creature, taking its time to deliver its intriguing medley of flavours and textures. Some compare this to the effect of a peacock's tail due to the way its different characters seem to unfurl gradually across the palate before finishing in a complex flourish that lingers dramatically.

Fresh and silky, the way Pinot Noir feels in the mouth definitely plays an important part in its appeal. In its youth it can offer an enticing aromatic bouquet of red fruits and florals, but with age it enters another dimension as it becomes more earthy, savoury and spicy.

Just as it's a variety that takes time and understanding to appreciate in the glass, it's also a bit of a prima donna in the vineyard. This sensitive plant only excels in cooler climates, and then only in the right spots and from vines that have had their fruit limited and attentively coaxed to display quality. It also demands kid-glove treatment in the winery if its promise is to be realised, requiring gentle handling and judicious use of the very best oak.

Given the attention to detail required, good Pinot Noir doesn't come cheap and you should be prepared to pay a bit more to ensure you avoid the bland examples that can be made at the lower end. However, as more Pinot comes onstream in New Zealand, prices are becoming competitive and it's now possible to purchase a decent drop for under $30.

France's Burgundy region (Bourgogne) is the spiritual home of the variety, where examples can vary in character within tiny areas and even between rows. This demonstrates how responsive it is to its situation, which is why the best tends to come from very specific spots rather than resulting from a regional blend. Difference is definitely something to be celebrated in this variety.

Other than Burgundy, in France it's also found in small outcrops in Alsace and the Loire. It's also one of the main grapes used in Champagne and many quality sparkling wines, where it is fermented without its skin to make a white wine (see page 83).

While many winemakers have tried to make it in unsuitably warm climates, more success has been achieved in Germany (where they call it Spätburgunder), Oregon (in the United States), Tasmania, some cooler sites in Chile and here in New Zealand,

> ‘I love Pinot Noir's ability to morph into a symphony that has all instruments playing in complete harmony.’
>
> Mike Eaton, TerraVin, Marlborough

which has swiftly gained recognition as one of the world's major quality Pinot players.

Swirl, sniff and slurp

Cherry, plum, raspberry, strawberry, violet, rose, mineral, spice, game, truffle, forest floor, fresh, silky, supple

> Cabernet Sauvignon, and the role it plays in Bordeaux blends, creates elegant, highly structured wines with a fruit spectrum from wild lavender through to ripe blackcurrants, delivering power and grace — a must-have for longevity.
>
> Kate Radburnd, CJ Pask, Hawke's Bay

CABERNET SAUVIGNON: Bordeaux's best
(CAB-er-NAY so-VEEN-yon)

An indisputably aristocratic grape variety that made its name through the châteaux of Bordeaux, Cabernet Sauvignon has a noble pedigree founded on the key part it's played in many of the greatest red wines of this region.

It can be a touch stern in its youth, with grippy tannins and tart acidity. This is why it's regularly blended with a softer, more early drinking companion such as Merlot, as in traditional Bordeaux blends. However, while it may take its time to open up, it can mellow magnificently with age, making some of the longest-lived reds.

Cabernet Sauvignon makes full-bodied wines, which while rich have a definite freshness to them. The fruit is on the darker end of the spectrum, with blackcurrant (or cassis in French) often noted, especially in examples from warmer climates. The oak barrels in which it is often aged add notes of cedar and cigar box.

Given their very different personalities, it's hard to accept that Cabernet Sauvignon is actually the offspring of the white variety

Sauvignon Blanc and its red Bordeaux blend companion, Cabernet Franc. Its white mother has left her imprint in the form of the green character that the variety can exhibit, which ranges from attractive olive and dried herb notes through to less appealing herbaceous, stalky and green-capsicum notes in examples made from grapes that were not sufficiently ripe.

These less desirable nuances, coupled with the astringent tannins that are also another symptom of unripe Cabernet, used to be found all too frequently in New Zealand Cabernets. A moderate amount of heat is needed for the grapes to ripen and reveal their regal magic, and with conditions somewhat marginal here, this hasn't always happened. However, on selected warmer sites, such as Hawke's Bay's Gimblett Gravels, and in warmer years, New Zealand can definitely make classy Cabs, although as a variety it is now in decline here.

While New Zealand is at the coolest climatic edge for growing Cabernet, the variety has been embraced by many other warmer regions beyond Bordeaux and can now be found around the world. Notable quantities have been planted in Australia, where Coonawarra produces examples oozing with rich, supple blackcurrant fruit and a twist of mint and Margaret River is making fresh, fine and elegant examples.

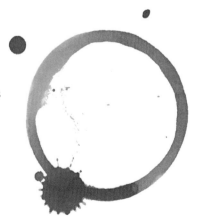

In California and Chile they make softer and more voluptuous versions, while in South Africa they can be more savoury and restrained. The Cabernet Sauvignon grape also grows well in Eastern Europe and Italy where it's been grown for years and, turns up in Sangiovese-based blends, as well as on its own, most notably in the iconic Sassicaia, one of Italy's top red wines.

Swirl, sniff and slurp

Blackcurrant, blackberry, black cherry, olive, mint, green capsicum, cedar, savoury, dried herb, leather, violets, cigar box, pencil shavings, mineral, earth, liquorice, dark chocolate, spice, full-bodied, grippy, juicy

SYRAH/SHIRAZ: so good they named it twice
(SI-rah/SHI-raz)

Given its engaging character it's no surprise that in recent years Syrah — or Shiraz as it's known in Australia and most other New World winemaking countries — has rapidly risen up the globe's grapevine charts. Voluptuously textured, sweetly fruited and with a spicy edge, it's gained fans hooked on its soft and fruity everyday examples as well as those looking for something more serious and structured.

Plums and boysenberries abound in the rich and softly textured Shirazes from Australia, often accompanied with spice and cedar from the new oak with which the grape has a great affinity. In cooler regions, such as its Rhône homeland in France, the fruit from this variety covers more of a raspberry and redcurrant spectrum, with aromatics redolent of white or black pepper. This black pepper note celebrated in some of its finest examples has recently been given scientific support with the discovery that Syrah actually shares a compound with black peppercorns!

In France, Syrah has often been overlooked in the hype

surrounding red Bordeaux and Burgundy. However, a new wave of forward-thinking producers in the northern Rhône has been propelling the region's stunning Syrahs back onto the world's prestige wine stage. However, over the last decade, the fourfold increase in its area in France has been largely driven by plantings in the warm southern Languedoc-Roussillon region. Here it makes ripe, fruit-driven and very affordable versions of the variety. It also regularly appears alongside the likes of Grenache and Mourvèdre in southern Rhône blends.

New World wine-producing countries have witnessed a similar Syrah explosion, with plantings in California, Chile and South Africa soaring. However, it's Australia, which boasts some of the world's oldest Shiraz vines, that has become the country most associated with the variety. Here its fullest, most sweetly fruited expression is to be found. With the exploration of cooler sites along with more sensitive winemaking, the variety's original oaky and alcoholic blockbusting styles have been joined by more refined and elegant examples.

New Zealand's Syrah has also started to turn heads of late, inspiring some envious looks from across the Tasman. We've more than doubled our area of Syrah in recent years following its success in warmer regions, especially Hawke's Bay, where it has been found to ripen more reliably than Cabernet Sauvignon and make elegant mid-weight Rhône-like examples perfumed with black pepper over fresh berry fruits.

Swirl, sniff and slurp

Plum, damson, boysenberry, cherry, blackberry, raspberry,

GOING AROUND THE BLEND

In these star-struck times, it's often wines made from a single variety that hog the limelight. However, some of the most famed wines are team efforts crafted with a number of different grapes: think Bordeaux, Chianti and Rioja, with Châteauneuf-du-Pape sometimes including a phenomenal 13 varieties!

This spread can help the winemaker cope with the vagaries of a vintage, where one variety might perform better than another in certain years. A varied palette of ingredients can also be used to enhance each variety's strengths and mask any weaknesses.

For example, in a Bordeaux, often austere Cabernet Sauvignon is used to provide structure and longevity; the reliably ripe Cabernet Franc comes to the fore in years when Cabernet Sauvignon struggles to ripen; Merlot adds a soft fleshiness, while Malbec brings colour.

A combination of red and white grapes can be found in some blends, such as the trendy assemblage du jour, Shiraz/Syrah with a splash of Viognier, which has taken off in Australia and increasingly here in New Zealand.

redcurrant, spice, black pepper, cedar, smoke, incense, meat, earthy, smooth

MERLOT: soft survivor
(MUR-low)

'If anyone orders Merlot, I'm leaving. I am not drinking any f-----g *Merlot!*' exclaims Miles, the main character in the American film *Sideways*, in which Merlot is much maligned. However, he's later seen knocking back a treasured bottle of Bordeaux, a Cheval Blanc that ironically contains a not insignificant proportion of Merlot, illustrating the two almost contradictory faces of this variety.

On the one hand, Merlot is responsible for crowd-pleasing easy-drinking everyday quaffers. On the other, it plays an important part in some of the world's most coveted wines. And while it may not provoke the same passion as Pinot Noir or have the power of Cabernet Sauvignon, with its soft sweet fruit and often voluptuous velvety texture, it still has plenty going for it, which makes Miles' censure of the variety seem as unfair as it is hypocritical.

When not treated seriously by those who make it, Merlot can indeed be rather ordinary. However, Miles' misgivings, along with those shared by other wine snobs, are most likely connected to its general popularity, combined with the fact that Merlot frequently plays a supporting role. As one of the most widely consumed red wine varieties in a number of countries, including the United States, it may just be too common for some!

Behind its wide-reaching allure is the approachability of its early drinking fleshy, creamy, textured fruit that can make for plump and pleasing wines. Its texture also makes it adept at filling in gaps left by other varieties or in smoothing the tougher edges of firmer grapes like Cabernet Sauvignon; something that has made it an important grape in blends.

In Bordeaux, Cabernet Sauvignon may have the star status, but it's Merlot that's actually the most planted grape variety. Here it produces some stunning wines with immense purity and richness. Its dominant presence in blends from St Émilion and Pomerol provides proof of its ability to age into something irresistibly savoury and earthy.

Merlot is more readily adaptable to a range of climates than the likes of Pinot Noir and Cabernet Sauvignon, which has seen it spread across the globe to become one of the world's most-planted varieties, and the number-two red grape in New Zealand.

Merlot's global success shows no sign of slowing. It remains one of the most popular varieties in the world and indeed in the United States, despite the *Sideways* sideswipe.

Swirl, sniff and slurp

Plum, blackberry, black cherry, milk chocolate, coffee, sweet spice, soft, smooth, velvety

Reds Less Travelled

GARNACHA/GRENACHE: sun worshipper
(gar-NASHA/Gr-NASH)

This Mediterranean heat seeker basks in the dry sunny climes of southern France, northern Spain, southern Italy and increasingly in Australia, California and South Africa.

Originating in Spain, Garnacha is the country's most widely planted red grape. It is the main variety in Navarra, is part of many Rioja blends, as well as being found in the exciting and intense reds of Priorat and in Spain's most revered red, Vega Sicilia. From Spain it has spread north into southern France and the southern Rhône, where it plays an important role in the region's blends.

Garnacha — known as Grenache in France — is also utilised in the production of rosé, found in the famous rosés of Provence and rosados of Spain.

Under its French name it is widely planted in the warm regions of Australia, but doesn't get much recognition there as it is often part of a blend. However, with the rise the GSM (the Grenache/Shiraz/Mourvèdre) blend, its presence is now more widely being acknowledged on wine labels and subsequently in the minds of drinkers of Australian wine.

With its light colour, low acid, high alcohol, soft tannins and relatively short shelf life, it does tend to work better in a blend than as a stand-alone variety. However, in its highest forms it can make quite intense and densely dark berry-fruited wines through to lighter red-fruited versions carrying its characteristic white pepper signature.

Swirl, sniff and slurp

White pepper, spice, strawberry, raspberry, blackberry, soft

CABERNET FRANC: frankly fragrant
(CAB-er-NAY FRONK)

Cabernet Franc's a sociable sort. Its somewhat slight frame needs to be filled out by more robust types, meaning it's rarely seen on its own, apart from in wines made in the French regions of Chinon and Bourgueil in the Loire Valley. It's mainly found fraternising with other varieties in traditional Bordeaux blends where it adds fragrance and freshness.

Lighter bodied than its offspring Cabernet Sauvignon, on its own it exhibits redcurrant and raspberry fruit, often with a green capsicum nuance in cooler climates. However, fruit in its riper incarnations from warmer regions or countries tends to be of a darker-berried nature.

Swirl, sniff and slurp

Dark fruit, redcurrant, raspberry, green capsicum, herb, fresh

THE RED WINE HEADACHE

While general over-indulgence is the culprit when it comes to the majority of wine-related headaches, these can be brought on in some people by a reaction to histamine, found at higher levels in red wines than in white.

MALBEC: dark horse
(MAL-beck)

With its intense inky black colour, Malbec is definitely one wine you don't want to be spilling on your Sunday best. A full body, dark berry fruit, notes of tar and leather, along with fairly chewy tannins are its major attributes.

Although it's another member of the Bordeaux-blend clan in which it plays a minor role, it's in the southern French region of Cahors where it made its name from its intense 'black wines', as they're known there.

More recently it's really taken off in Argentina where it produces a softer and fleshier wine, often with lots of intense but fresh dark plum and mulberry fruit. Its success has led it to becoming Argentina's most widely planted variety, and has established it as the country's flagship grape.

Some single varietal Malbecs are also being grown in warmer parts of New Zealand, although much ends up in Bordeaux blends.

Swirl, sniff and slurp

Dark berry fruit, tar, leather, spice, violets, smooth, velvety

TEMPRANILLO: Spanish flyer
(TEMP-ra-NEE-oh)

With the current trend for all things Spanish, Tempranillo is a grape that's been gaining popularity. It's the main quality grape in Rioja and is responsible under various different names for wines across Spain. Tasting of strawberries in its youthful examples, through to something altogether spicier and savoury in oak-aged and older expressions, some Tempranillo has now been planted in New Zealand and the resulting first wines suggest promise for the variety.

Swirl, sniff and slurp

Strawberry, raspberry, spice, herb, vanilla, earthy, leather, soft

SANGIOVESE: by Jove!

(SAN-jo-VAY-zee)

Among Italy's treasure trove of indigenous varieties, Sangiovese (the literal translation is the blood of Jove) is widely grown and is the mainstay of one of its most famous wines, Chianti. It's also behind Brunello di Montalcino, Vino Nobile di Montepulciano and a key ingredient of the Super Tuscan wines.

This divine liquid takes many forms, from lighter examples with juicy cherry fruit and herbal notes to weightier wines with darker fruit and a savoury spicy character.

Growers outside Italy — in Australia and California, with tiny quantities also being grown in the warmer parts of New Zealand — have sought to emulate Italy's illustrious examples with some success, although few have achieved the same supple and savoury splendour of the Italian versions.

Swirl, sniff and slurp

Cherry, plum, strawberry, dried herb, savoury, earthy, spice, coffee, supple, fresh

NEBBIOLO: tar and roses
(NEB-ee-OH-low)

Vying with Sangiovese for the position of Italy's greatest grape is Nebbiolo, a wonderfully perfumed varietal whose aromas are often described as tar and roses. Its combination of high acid and high tannin can make it quite austere in its youth, but it becomes more approachable with the age this long-lived variety is able to attain.

Sadly, attempts to make great Nebbiolo beyond the hills of Piedmont, where it excels in the wines of Barolo and Barbaresco, have largely been unsuccessful, although this hasn't stopped winemakers in Australia and even now in New Zealand persevering and achieving occasionally satisfying results.

Swirl, sniff and slurp

Blackberry, cherry, floral/rose, truffle, toasty, tar, liquorice, leather, cigar box, fresh, chewy

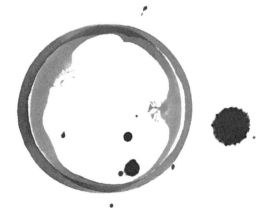

Other reds

Pinotage (PEE-noh-TARGE) may be in decline in New Zealand vineyards, but in South Africa, where some of the best examples are to be found, the popularity of this Pinot Noir-Cinsaut cross has made it the country's national grape. At its best it can offer a dense spicy mouthful of plums and blackberries while at its worst, it can make somewhat rustic and rubbery-tasting wines.

Covering Italy's many intriguing grape varieties would require another book altogether. However, Montepulciano (Mont-ee-PULCH-ee-AH-noh) is worth a mention; it's a grape with supple plummy fruit that's widely grown in that country, and there's even a little made here in New Zealand. Down in southern Italy there's Nero d'Avola (NARE-oh DAH-vo-LA), or the 'black grape of Avola', so called due to its deep colour and full-bodied dark berry fruit, and the spicy, plush and dark-berried Primitivo (Prim-ee-TEE-voh), which has been found to be the same grape as the Zinfandel (ZIN-fan-DELL) widely grown in the States.

THRILLS AND SPILLS

Why is it that whenever you spill some wine, it's almost always a full-bodied red? While I can't answer that question, I do have some suggestions for removing wine stains from your carpet. You must act quickly. Blot but don't scrub the affected area with paper towels. Douse the stain with water and continue blotting then diluting until the stain is removed. Stain removal products can be used on particularly stubborn stains, which should never be left to set.

"If we don't trial new grape varieties, we'll never know what works best."

John Hancock, Trinity Hill, Hawke's Bay

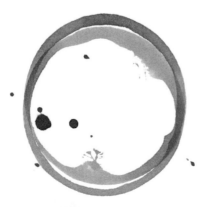

1

PINOT NOIR

Select an example from Marlborough where the competitive prices are now being matched by increasingly impressive quality.

SUGGESTED WINES

W5 Marlborough Pinot Noir, $15–20

Delta Vineyard Marlborough Pinot Noir, $20–26

Clayridge Marlborough Pinot Noir, $26–30

TASTING NOTE: What you've got in your glass should embody the variety's light and fresh personality. In simpler versions, Marlborough Pinot Noir is all plum and cherries, maybe with a hint of spice from some contact with oak. In more sophisticated examples, this can be joined by more savoury, forest floor and floral elements, which can linger in the mouth long after the wine has been swallowed.

2 MERLOT

SUGGESTED WINES

Ngatarawa Stables Hawke's Bay Merlot, $15–20
Mills Reef Reserve Hawkes Bay Merlot, $20–25
Craggy Range Gimblett Gravels Vineyard Merlot, $25–30

TASTING NOTE: Merlot's plum and dark berry fruit is often to the fore in its wines and you may be able to discern a chocolatey note. It can sometimes be quite chocolatey in texture too, given its soft and rich nature.

3

GARNACHA/GRENACHE

SUGGESTED WINES

Artazuri Navarra Garnacha, Spain, $15–20

Sorrento Dry Grown McLaren Vale Grenache, Australia
  $15–20

Grenache-based Côtes du Rhône blend such as Domaine de la
  Mordorée Côtes du Rhône, France, $20–25

TASTING NOTE: Another grape that makes softer reds with fruit that tends to be on the more red fruit spectrum of strawberry and raspberry, often identifiable by its white pepper notes. Grenache can be lighter in colour and body, although older vines can add depth and intensity.

SYRAH

Choose a local example that illustrates the cool-climate style.

SUGGESTED WINES

Elephant Hill Hawke's Bay Syrah, $20–25
Vidal Hawke's Bay Syrah, $25–30
Church Road Hawke's Bay Syrah, $30–36

TASTING NOTE: Cool-climate Syrahs like these can often be intensely aromatic, with quite overt notes of cracked black pepper, spice and incense that you should be able to pick up on the nose and palate. The fruit is at the darker end of the spectrum, supported by medium acidity and tannins.

5

CABERNET SAUVIGNON

Australia's Coonawarra Cabernet shows some of the variety's classic blackcurrant fruit character, often with a hint of mint or eucalypt.

SUGGESTED WINES

Rymill The Yearling Coonawarra Cabernet Sauvignon, Australia, $15–20

Richmond Grove Coonawarra Cabernet Sauvignon, Australia, $20–25

Hollick Coonawarra Cabernet Sauvignon, Australia, $25–30

TASTING NOTE: Your first sniff should yield an unmistakeable bouquet of blackcurrants, maybe with a hint of mint or eucalyptus. On the palate, you should find Cabernet to be full-bodied and concentrated, with fresh acidity and a bit of tannic grip. In the Coonawarra style, tannins tend to be quite ripe and supple, but are still in evidence.

6 PRIMITIVO

SUGGESTED WINES

Pasqua Lapaccio Salento Primitivo, Italy, $15–19

Quota 29 Salento Primitivo, Italy, $19–20

Sessantanni Primitivo Di Manduria, Italy, $20–40

TASTING NOTE: You'll see that this is almost opaque, with the wine's flavours as concentrated as its colour. There should be plenty of dark fruit, ranging from sweetly ripe to dried and pruney, sometimes accompanied by savoury undertones and notes of leather, tobacco and spice.

CHAPTER FOUR

Sparkling, Sweet and Stronger Stuff

'Wine has one simple responsibility: to be a medium for communication.'

Rudi Bauer, Quartz Reef, Central Otago

Fantastic fizz

It may seem surprising, but until the eighteenth century bubbles in Champagne were bad news. Makers of the famous French region's initially still wines fought the fizz caused by the re-fermentation process, which in the frail bottles of yore could have calamitously explosive consequences.

With the development of stronger bottles and the wire cage that prevented corks from popping prematurely, the sparkle that was to be key to Champagne's success became an element to be actively embraced rather than avoided.

While the term Champagne can only be applied to wine that comes from the northern French region of the same name, which fiercely protects the identity of the wines that have become synonymous with luxury and celebration, sparkling wines are now made throughout the world. The best hail from cooler areas with the right conditions to engender the light fresh wines required for the finest fizz.

BRINGING ON THE BUBBLES: how wines get their sparkle

Wine has been spontaneously re-fermenting since grapes and yeast first got together. However, winemakers have since sought to control this process leading to the development of a number of ways in which sparkling wines can be made.

It's the Méthode Traditionnelle developed in the Champagne region that's responsible for Champagne and the highest quality sparkling wines. In this procedure the wines are firstly fermented in a similar way to still wine, except the black grapes — traditionally Pinot Noir and Pinot Meunier — have their skins removed before they leave any trace of colour.

Batches of this still white wine are then combined using the art of assemblage, creating the desired style from a blend of many different vats or barrels, which is then put into bottles. Sparkling rosés incorporate a little red wine from black grapes fermented separately with their skins.

But it's not until a mixture of sugar, wine and yeast is added to this blend and the bottles capped with a temporary seal that the real magic starts. This process kicks off a second fermentation, trapping carbon dioxide in the bottles to create fizz.

Sparkling wines also gain complexity from the time they spend in contact with the dead yeast cells that have sunk down to the bottom of the bottle after they've done their work. The period the wines spend 'on lees', as this process is known, varies across sparkling wines, with a longer time resulting in a richer wine.

At this point the wine is quite cloudy from all that dead yeast. This is removed by a process that starts with something called riddling, where the bottles are gradually moved until they are in an upside-down vertical position, which causes the sediment to slide into the neck. This was originally a painstaking operation carried out by hand but, nowadays is more often performed by a machine known as a gyropalate that's been found to do the job just as well.

The next stage involves freezing the necks of the bottles so that when the bottles are righted and the caps removed, the plug of now-frozen yeast in each one pops out leaving the wine crystal clear. The bottles are then swiftly topped up with a wine-sugar mix, called the dosage, which determines the level of sweetness of the finished fizz. Then the cork is inserted, the cage secured and the bottle's good to go.

Méthode Traditionnelle is a canny and complicated procedure, which is why you pay a premium price for the time and effort involved. However, the end product is of the highest quality, with a finer mousse — the French term for the bubbles — plus more complexity and finesse.

Less costly techniques for making sparkling wine have also been developed outside the Champagne region. The highest quality alternative is the transfer method, which follows the same path as Méthode Traditionnelle until it comes to removing the yeast. This is achieved by transferring the contents of the whole bottle under pressure into a large tank, after which the wine is filtered in bulk and put into fresh bottles. The resulting bubbly is usually labelled 'bottle fermented' and while it can be of good quality, the bubbles are not quite as elegant as those produced by the Méthode Traditionnelle.

Another process used to make the majority of cheaper sparklers is the tank method, where the second fizz-inducing fermentation takes place in a sealed tank. While wines made in this way can be perfectly acceptable, they lack the complexity of wine made by the previous two methods and their bubbles tend to be bigger and shorter-lived.

Carbonation — the same process used for making fizzy drinks

— is the crudest method of giving wine some spritz. It results in the biggest but briefest bubbles and is only used in the very cheapest wines.

CHAMPAGNE AND BEYOND

In any conversation about sparkling wine, Champagne will be the name fizzing on the tip of most tongues. A relatively small, demarcated area in northeastern France, the Champagne region's small size, coupled with its reputation for making the world's best bubbles, means you pay the highest price for its wines.

Champagne's finesse lies in the combination of the coolness of the region and its chalky soils. However, its marginality as a grape-growing region brings with it risks of unripeness, rot and minuscule harvests. These vagaries of vintage led the region's winemakers to start blending grapes from different vineyards and different years for greater consistency in quality and style, a method subsequently adopted in other parts of the world. These non-vintage wines (NV) make up the highest percentage of the Champagne region's production. When Mother Nature smiles on the cool hills of Champagne, these best years are the ones in which vintage Champagne is made.

While Champagne is still regarded as the *ne plus ultra* of sparkling wines, with the best products of the region still unparalleled in quality, it's possible to make beautiful bubbles elsewhere. In other regions of France, sparkling wines known as *crémants* can provide simpler and more affordable options, as do other traditional sparkling wines such as Cava in Spain and

UNDER PRESSURE

The pressure inside a sparkling wine bottle is easily as high as that in a car tyre, making it possible for the cork to be propelled from the bottle at 40 km/hour — so it's definitely worth standing back when you pop that cork!

Prosecco and the sweet low-alcohol Asti in Italy.

In the Southern Hemisphere, Australia is producing some fine fizz in the cooler regions of Victoria and Tasmania, including its own singular style, the big sweetish sparkling Shiraz. Meanwhile, in New Zealand, which has a climate particularly suited to sparklers, we're arguably making some of the world's best everyday bubbly — as well as serious stuff made by a handful of producers committed to this time-consuming form of winemaking.

Even in ultra-chilly England they're positively effervescing over the quality of their sparkling wines. In fact, some Champagne houses have been buying land for vineyards there, due to concerns that global warming could one day make Champagne too hot for the best bubbles!

SPARKLING STYLES

ULTRA BRUT, EXTRA BRUT, BRUT NATURE, BRUT SAUVAGE, BRUT ZERO, ZERO DOSAGE: an increasingly fashionable style where no sugar has been added, making it almost bone dry

BRUT: very dry: the most popular style

EXTRA SEC/EXTRA DRY: pretty dry, but not as dry as Brut

SEC: off dry

DEMI-SEC: sweet

DOUX, DOLCE: lusciously sweet

BLANC DE BLANCS: made from 100% Chardonnay, which tends to produce a lighter, racier style

BLANC DE NOIRS: a white sparkler made from black grapes only, which tends to produce a fuller bodied wine

PRESTIGE CUVÉE: the top wine produced by many Champagne houses and blended from the finest wines. Most, but not all, of these are vintage wines

Swirl, sniff and slurp

Bread, yeast, apple, citrus, mineral, raspberry, cream, vanilla, sweet pastry

Just desserts

Rich and rare, unctuous and often unbelievably difficult to produce, sweet wines, stickies, dessert wines — call them what you will — are some of the most exquisite wines of all. However, dessert wines are sadly also some of the most under-appreciated and overlooked styles. This is largely due to the erroneous notion that sweet means unsophisticated, combined with their place at the end of the meal when appetites are sated and sweet wine options all too often forgotten.

While some dessert wines are made from grapes that have been left to get ultra-ripe on the vine, many of the best derive their characteristic sweetness and intensity from the deliberate raisining (or drying) of grapes. In the case of Italy's Recioto and Vin Santo wines, grapes are actually dried after picking. However, the majority of the world's great 'sweeties' are raisined on the vine, with their nectareous nature bestowed upon them . . . by a rot!

WHAT ROT?

Called botrytis, this Jekyll and Hyde character can reduce grapes to a mushy mess in its malevolent form (known as grey rot). However, on the right grapes at the right time, it becomes 'noble', a word you'll often see on the labels of bottles where this fungus has worked its wonders on the contents.

The botrytis causes healthy grapes to shrivel, which concentrates their sugar while leaving their acid relatively intact, and the affected bunches, or sometimes even single grapes, are then hand-selected, often in a number of sorties through the vineyard.

These deeply unattractive, mouldy-looking bunches belie the riches they eventually yield: ultra-sweet and richly flavoured wines with notes of marmalade, citrus peel, honey and spice, which retain a fantastic freshness that prevents the wines from being cloying.

Botrytis loves damp conditions, making those vineyards located near bodies of water such as lakes or rivers particularly suited to growing grapes destined to be made into stickies. Here the grapes are often left on the vine — long after those for table wines have been harvested — to become ultra-ripe and raisined.

Sweet wines straddle various styles. In Germany, home to some of the most distinguished noble Rieslings, the styles range from the lighter late harvest Auslese wines, which may contain some botrytis-affected grapes, through to the riper and likely more botrytis-infused Beerenauslese (BA) to the rare, amazingly rich and heavily botrytised Trockenbeerenauslese (TBA).

Germany, along with Austria and Canada, also makes another ultra-sweet style called Eiswein. Instead of botrytis concentrating

a grape's sugars, in Eiswein freezing serves the same purpose. Thus frozen grapes are picked and pressed immediately, with the water crystals left behind in the press — and the sweetest juice, which has a lower freezing point than water, becomes the end product.

In France, noble rot plays its part in the sumptuously sweet Sémillon-Sauvignon Blanc blend of Sauternes, as well as often more affordable alternatives from Monbazillac, Côteaux du Layon and Alsace's Sélection de Grains Nobles wines (literally 'selection of noble berries').

In Hungary, Tokaji is a botrytised wine made in a unique way that uses non-affected grapes to make a dry base wine, to which a sweet paste made from botrytis-affected grapes (known as Aszú) is added in proportions measured out in puttonyos (the traditional baskets or hods that contain the paste). The number of puttonyos on the bottle's label indicates sweetness, with one the driest and six the sweetest.

In its coastal regions, New Zealand has maritime climes suited to stickie production and in favourable years these have been the source of a sumptuous selection of noble Rieslings, Sémillons and even Sauvignons.

Making sweet wines is a risky and time-consuming business, often resulting in only minuscule quantities being made from the small amounts of super-concentrated juice extracted from the raisined grapes. Such a process can make sweet wines expensive to buy, but many are worth every golden drop.

Although often defined as dessert wines, it's a myth that they must be consumed with that course of a meal. While pairing such a wine with pudding can create a heavenly union, they're also a great alternative to dessert, with many of them warranting their own occasion.

Swirl, sniff and slurp

Marmalade, citrus zest, lemon, honey, spice, apricot, peach, candied peel, blossom, caramel, toffee, nut

Fortify yourself

Fortified wines — those to which some spirit has been added — encompass some of the great wine styles of the world. Think Spain and the salty sherries of Jerez; or Portugal and the luscious ports of the Douro Valley; or the rich liqueur wines to be found in Australia's Rutherglen.

However, in New Zealand, fortified wines have been having a particularly hard time of late. Not only have they fallen out of favour following the legacy of flagons filled with less than enthralling liquid, they were also taxed into near oblivion recently when excise rates on alcoholic drinks over 14% near doubled.

The excise hikes decimated New Zealand's fortified wine industry. However, those who hung in there or started producing quality versions for the more discerning drinker are making some impressive wines. And while the tax makes imported fortified wine more expensive, there's still a diminutive but decent selection coming into the country.

STORMING PORT

You don't have to be posh or know which way to pass it (clockwise, if you really want to know) to appreciate the sweet, rich and warming character of port, the classic fortified wine of Portugal. It is created from fortifying a full-bodied sweet wine with spirit before all its sugar is turned into alcohol.

While the thought of folk thrusting their feet among the grapes may sound a little off-putting in these sanitised times, the traditional practice of foot treading plays an important part in the production of the finest ports. Although mechanised crushing is now more common, the gentle pressure exerted by the human hoof on port's grapes remains ideal for extracting maximum colour from their skins and minimum bitterness from their pips.

After being fortified to an alcoholic strength of around 20%, ports are then crafted in a variety of styles. Ruby is the simplest and cheapest, which is bottled young when it's still fruity and fiery. Tawny port comes in different guises, with the cheaper ones often just lighter-coloured ruby quality wines. Aged tawnies on the other hand, which you can identify by an age statement on the label, have spent considerable time in a cask, where they develop a wonderfully soft, spicy and complex character.

Vintage is the top of the port quality pyramid, constituting some of the world's most long-lived wines. Released only from the best years and best sites, vintage ports spend only a short time in a cask, requiring many further years in the bottle to soften.

For those after a more affordable and ready-to-drink vintage option, Late Bottled Vintage (LBV) is a good choice. As this

People tend to associate port with winter, but the tawny style actually lends itself to being chilled, making it well suited to summer drinking.

description suggests, it comes from a single year, but is far softer and less intense than vintage.

Swirl, sniff and slurp

Berries, dark fruit, spice, nut, cocoa, dried fruit, fig, prune, liquorice, chocolate

SHERRY BABY

Impostors masquerading as sherry are sadly often the first and — for some — the last experience some people have of this fine fortified wine whose authentic examples can only be made in the Jerez region of southern Spain. It's head and shoulders above the homegrown products that many have encountered, made from the addition of a slug of spirit to a dodgy sweet wine. True sherry is the often-refined result of a long and complex ageing process.

Unlike port, most sherries are dry wines when they're fortified. Sweeter styles, often sold as 'cream', are created by the addition of sweet wines made from sun-dried Pedro Ximénez and Moscatel grapes, which on their own make the only naturally sweet wines of Jerez.

The secret of sherry's unique style lies within the solera, a dynamic system of fractional blending. After being made into a dry table wine, sherries are classified by the kind of character the winemaker feels they suggest in terms of style, before being fortified with grape brandy to differing degrees depending on the desired end style. They're then put into the first tier of barrels in the system, before being gradually transferred up through this multi-layered stack over a minimum period of three years and often much longer, until they reach the final row when they're drawn off for bottling.

Finos and the stylistically similar Manzanilla (made specifically in the sub-region, Sanlúcar de Barrameda) are the lightest and palest sherries, shaped by the spontaneous presence of a veil of yeasts called flor living on the surface of the wine. The flor consumes alcohol and prevents oxidation, leaving a fresh, tangy, slightly lower strength sherry, with a distinctive yeasty, almost salty character.

Finos that have lost their flor, turn into a different style known as Amontillado. Without that protective blanket of yeast, this style of sherry turns amber and develops more nutty notes. Even darker is the style known as Oloroso, which never had any flor to begin with and which consequently becomes deep brown through contact with the air, making for a full, intense and savoury style.

For wine drinkers more familiar with the fruit-driven flavours of most of the wines on the market, the first sip of a real sherry can be something of a surprise. Rather than fruit, the attraction of these wines lies in their more savoury dimension, with notes of nut and spice. Open your mind and prepare to be seduced!

Swirl, sniff and slurp

Chalky, yeast, savoury, nutty, dried fruit, walnut, salty, raisin, citrus peel

LIQUEUR LOVELIES

Closer to home, some of the most decadent and distinctive fortified wines can be found across the Tasman. Almost Christmas cake in liquid form, Rutherglen's liqueur wines ooze raisiny richness.

These are made from grapes that have been left to shrivel on the vine. Like port, the resulting wine is fortified before much of the sugar has been fermented. This supremely sweet wine is then stored in oak casks for years, gaining complexity and concentration through a process of slow evaporation. Some are aged in a way similar to sherry (in a solera system), while others are drawn from a master blend made up of the best barrels selected from a mix of vintages.

Muscat, known as Frontignac in Australia, is regarded as the greatest grape for this style, producing incredibly rich and syrupy wines with intense dried fruit, nutty and toffee flavours. Made in four styles, these ascend in richness, complexity and rarity from the foundation style simply called Rutherglen Muscat, to Classic Rutherglen Muscat, Grand Rutherglen Muscat and finally Rare Rutherglen Muscat.

Rutherglen's other great liqueur wine is made from the Muscadelle grape, which produces lighter and more subtly flavoured sweet wines. Traditionally called Tokay, it has recently been renamed Topaque due to similarities between Tokay and the Hungarian Tokaji. Along with other names taken from European appellations, such as sherry and port, Tokay had to be dropped from labels following a trade agreement between Australia and the European Union.

Swirl, sniff and slurp

Dried fruit, fruitcake, nut, coffee, toffee, caramel, molasses, marmalade, fig, vanilla, caramel, butterscotch

1 SPARKLING WINE

SUGGESTED WINES

Lindauer Brut Cuvée NV, $15–20
Quartz Reef Méthode Traditionnelle Central Otago NV, $25–30
Lanvin & Fils Brut Champagne NV, France, $40–50

TASTING NOTE: First look at the bubbles. The smaller and more persistent, the better the wine, which should be supported by the evidence of your first sip. But before doing this, take on board its aromas of apple, citrus and yeasty sometimes almost Marmitey notes. When tasting the wine you'll notice its mouth-watering acidity, often balanced by a hint of sweetness, with examples that have spent more time maturing exhibiting bready and sweet pastry notes.

2
FINO/MANZANILLA SHERRY

SUGGESTED WINES

Gonzalez Byass Elegante Dry Palomino Fino, Spain, $25–30

Hidalgo Manzanilla Pasada Pastrana Single Vineyard
  Manzanilla, Spain, $35–40

Valdespino Inocente Single Vineyard Fino (375ml), Spain,
  $20–25

TASTING NOTE: Yeasty notes can also be found on both the nose and palate of Fino and Manzanilla sherries from the flor that has been protecting them. The nose can be quite pungent and the palate tangy with notes of apple and almond and sometimes a suggestion of saltiness.

3 NOBLE DESSERT WINE

SUGGESTED WINES

Saints Vineyard selection Gisborne Noble Semillon (375ml),
  $20–25
Glazebrook Regional Reserve Hawke's Bay Noble Harvest
  Riesling (375ml), $30–35
Carmes de Rieussec Sauternes (375ml), France, $30–35

TASTING NOTE: Spot the wonderfully golden hue from the effect of the noble rot, botrytis. Give the wine a sniff and you should be able to smell botrytis's hallmark marmalade note, which you'll go on to taste along with apricots, peaches and honey. Incredibly viscous and sweet, its kick of citrusy acidity makes its finish quite fresh.

4

PORT/PORT STYLE

SUGGESTED WINES

Quinta de la Rosa Ruby Port, Portugal, $35–40

Trinity Hill Hawkes Bay 'Port', $40–45

Graham's LBV, Portugal, $45–50

TASTING NOTE: Dark berries and spice should be in abundance on the nose and palate, sometimes accompanied by fig and chocolaty notes and a seasoning of spice. It's pretty sweet and you should be able to feel the heat from its higher alcohol level, which can give cheaper examples a fiery quality. Better ones are smooth and rich, with a touch of tannin.

5 MADEIRA

As very little Madeira comes into New Zealand, there's not a huge variety to choose from. However, to get an idea of the sweetest richest style, go for the following example or one with 'Malmsey' on the label.

SUGGESTED WINE

Blandy's Duke of Clarence Rich Madeira, $50–55

TASTING NOTE: This is almost fruitcake in a glass, with dried fruit and spice on both nose and its mid-weight palate — and some nuts in there, too. This style is sweet but still pleasantly fresh, with lots of intensity and flavours that really linger.

6 LIQUEUR MUSCAT

SUGGESTED WINE

Morris Liqueur Muscat, (500ml) Australia, $20–25

Campbells Rutherglen Muscat, (375ml) Australia, $20–25

De Bortoli Show Reserve Liqueur Muscat, (750ml) Australia,
   $45–50

TASTING NOTE: Let those wonderful aromas of candied peel
and fruitcake waft past your nostrils before taking a sip of the
sweetest of stickies. You'll be tasting lots of dried fruits, such
as raisins and dates, with notes of vanilla and spice.

CHAPTER FIVE

The Human Touch

'Winemaking is the miracle of assemblage — the blending
of different varieties from different sites to achieve a complexity
that is not present in the separate components.'

John Buck, Te Mata Estate, Hawke's Bay

Wine is one of the few alcoholic beverages that technically does not require any input from humans. However, without a human hand to guide the process, the fruits of these spontaneous ferments remain pretty rough stuff and quickly degrade into vinegar.

It's been speculated that Man may have been making wine as early as Neolithic times, although vin de Stone Age Man would bear little resemblance to the refined examples we drink today. What we put in our glasses is the product of thousands of years of fine-tuning that's moved winemaking from an enterprise that employed more luck than judgement to a modern science in which most of its processes are understood and controlled.

You'll often hear it said that great wine is made in the vineyard. While no great wine has ever been made from bad grapes, what happens in the winery enables great grapes to express their full potential in the final wine.

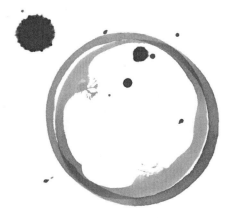

Red, white or rosé? How wine is made

Stripped back to its basics, wine is a relatively simple affair in which a grape's sugars are converted by yeasts to alcohol and the by-product, carbon dioxide. How this is managed and the way a wine is subsequently treated has, however, a major impact on the character of the final wine.

White wine is usually made from white grapes that have been crushed, their skins removed and the juice fermented. Given the delicate nature of their flavours, most are shielded from contact with potentially destructive oxygen and fermented at lower temperatures.

Before this approach was widely employed, white wines, especially from warmer regions, often lacked fruit and freshness. One of the major leaps in white-wine quality came with the widespread adoption of temperature-controlled vats, which was largely responsible for the end of tired and tasteless whites.

In the case of red wines, after crushing, the skins are left in with the wine throughout the fermentation. As the juice of almost all black grapes is actually colourless, it's this contact with the skins where all the pigments reside that gives red wine its colour, as well as tannin. After fermentation, the winemaker may choose to keep the wine in with its skins until sufficient colour and tannin have been extracted before it's run off for blending, bottling or maturing in barrels.

A rosé's pink hue is brought about in a variety of ways. It's rare in a quality wine for a red to be added to a white to create a pink wine, although this is the case when making Champagne. More often rosés start out being made the same way as red wines, but the skins are removed after a far shorter period and the wine goes on to

WINEMAKER SPEAK

When using technical terms it can sometimes seem as if winemakers are speaking a foreign language. Here is some of the specialised lingo that can find its way into back labels and tasting notes.

YIELD: this is the amount of actual or potential grapes harvested from a specified area. In general, the lower the yield the more concentrated and consequently higher quality the wine. Grapes such as Pinot Noir are particularly sensitive to yield, which must be kept low in quality wines.

BRIX: a measurement of grape sugars used to judge ripeness and potential alcohol.

TA: these initials stands for total acidity in a wine, with high levels indicating a crisp wine and low levels suggesting something softer.

RS: the initials for residual sugar or the amount of sugar left in a final bottled wine that provides an idea of its sweetness: under 3g/l (grams per litre) is virtually dry; over 10g/l off dry; over 200g/l will take a wine into the ultra-sweet dessert spectrum.

PARCEL: usually refers to a batch of grapes grown in the same small area.

be fermented like a white wine.

This is the bare essentials of how wine is made. However, there are many other ways a winemaker can intervene during and after fermentation to shape a wine further.

OPTIONAL EXTRAS: oak and other influences

Like an artist, the winemaker can choose to draw out certain nuances in their subject and add touches of their own. However, while the makers of liqueurs and spirits could be regarded more like abstract painters in that they heavily manipulate their material through the addition of flavourings, the winemaker is more of a realist, working to subtly enhance what nature has provided them with.

One of the main ways a winemaker can influence wine lies in their choice of fermentation vessel, which can affect both a wine's flavour and texture. A stainless steel tank imparts no flavour, but being airtight it will preserve fruit and freshness.

Oak barrels, however, let in tiny amounts of oxygen that can soften wine and increase the complexity of its flavours and add to its weight and impart tannins which are a natural preservative that can help a wine to age. They can also impart woody flavours to a wine, the strongest coming from new barriques to almost nothing from older and larger vessels. Different kinds of oak also add different nuances, with American oak being the most overt, often adding coconutty and vanilla notes, while French oak can add more restrained cedar and spice notes.

AVOIDING OAK

If you think you don't like the taste of oak, it may be that you can't stomach its overuse. Employed judiciously it can add texture and subtle spice to a wine, but many wine drinkers have written it off through experiencing excessively oaky examples where it's overwhelmed the fruit. If you really can't stand it, choose a Chardonnay labelled unwooded or varieties such as Sauvignon Blanc and Riesling that tend to be oak-free. With reds it's harder to tell as most of these could potentially have seen some oak, but descriptors such as spicy, cedar and mocha are a giveaway that a tree has played a part in its production.

Another aspect of winemaking that can be manipulated is the malolactic fermentation process. All red wines undergo this conversion of the harsher malic acid that is also found in apples and present in all wine, to the softer lactic acid one tastes in milk. However, in whites it can be avoided to create crisper styles, or encouraged to create softer fatter wines, often displaying a buttery note as found in many Chardonnays.

Blending is a vitally important part of winemaking. It's more of a creative art than a science in which the winemaker uses taste and tactile perception to select complementary wines often from dozens of different vessels to create the final blend that's to be bottled.

Many wines are blends. Some use wines from a single vineyard, while others combine multiple vineyards, regions or varieties (see page 65).

Winemakers also have the option of adding certain permitted additives to a wine as it's being made to affect its quality and stability. One of the most important of these is sulphur dioxide (SO_2) — already present in tiny quantities in the grapes — which has been used for centuries by winemakers to preserve wines and protect them from spoilage by bacteria or oxidation.

At the end of fermentation many wines need a touch of tidying up to present them in the clear and stable state to which the modern wine drinker has become accustomed. To remove particles that if left could make a wine cloudy, harsh or exhibit off flavours, many wines are filtered and fined.

When filtered, wines are passed through membranes that trap matter, while fining uses various agents — usually natural protein extracts — that attract unwanted molecules. Only negligible amounts of these agents, if any, remain in the final wine, and range from the classic egg-white fining regularly used for red and higher quality wines to isinglass from the swim bladder of a fish used in many whites. Gelatine, made from animal bones and tissues, is one of the more aggressive agents, which tends to be used on the cheapest products such as cask wine.

Finding closure: cork or screwcap?

When a wine is ready to go out into the world, it is bottled. But the winemaker has another major decision still to make in the way the bottle will be sealed.

Natural cork has been the traditional stopper for wine since the 1600s, when it was adopted by the French monk Dom Pérignon to replace the flighty cloth-wrapped wooden plugs that kept popping out of his Champagne containers. Prized for the compressibility that enables it to make the near-airtight seal required to stop wine oxidising, cork soon came to be the world's most widely used wine closure.

However, cork has not been without its issues. These primarily stem from a malodorous mould called TCA (2,4,6-trichloroanisole to give it its technical name) found in cork bark and which imparts musty aromas and flavours to a wine. Since the arrival of alternatives, the cork industry has started to clean up its act, and at long last corks appear to have improved.

TCA isn't the only issue with cork, which as a natural product has an inherent variability. While some provide the tight seal required to stop wine-destroying oxygen into the bottle, others let some sneak past, which can lead to oxidation and variation between different bottles of the same wine stoppered with cork.

Natural cork is just one option however. Synthetic (plastic) corks have been used with some success on wines for early drinking, while the cork-based closure Diam is being used on a growing number of red wines in New Zealand. Diam is constructed from tiny particles of cork dust from which the TCA present has been zapped by the same technology used to decaffeinate coffee.

However, the closure that's swiftly established itself as the main alternative to cork is the screwcap, especially in New Zealand where it now stoppers an estimated 90% of our wines. As well as being a sterile closure with a reliable seal, the fact that screwcaps make wine so darned easy to open has won followers who have been casting corkscrews aside in their droves.

VIN NATUREL VERSUS FRANKENSTEIN WINE

There's no denying that technology has ushered in huge improvements to winemaking. Not only are the wines available today better, but it's also now possible to make a drinkable wine out of grapes that previously may not have been considered useable thanks to new techniques that allow winemakers much more control over their fruit.

Given wine is considered a natural product, people are often surprised to discover the number of additives that can often be involved. Wines can be tweaked or sometimes downright transformed by the addition of acid, sugar and tannins or use of processes such as reverse osmosis to reduce alcohol levels and micro-oxygenation to soften wines more quickly than conventional barrel ageing. Are these Frankenstein wines and just how much manipulation is acceptable?

These additions can speed up the winemaking process or deal with issues arising from less-than-perfect grapes. While most people wouldn't be able to pick up their presence in the final wine, purists and proponents of a natural approach argue it's better to get things right in the vineyard first to avoid the need for tinkering later.

There has also been a growing interest in returning to more traditional winemaking techniques. For its exponents, modern winemaking can turn out wines that are just too homogenised and 'squeaky clean', focused on fruit rather than more complex characters and texture; such winemakers are prepared to cede some control to give nature a freer rein over their ferments.

One hands-off approach increasingly embraced in a growing number of top wines is allowing the wine to be fermented by the wild (or indigenous) yeasts that build up naturally in wineries and vineyards where wine has been made for some time. Using cultured yeasts has become the norm due to their reliability in contrast to indigenous yeasts that like to do their own thing, which can include giving up before the ferment has finished or working incredibly slowly.

VEGETARIAN WINE

Those wanting to make an ethical choice are largely left in the dark by our current wine labelling laws, which only require wineries to list allergens, such as egg, fish and milk-based fining products. Any wine that says it's been left unfined is a safe bet for vegetarians, and dead certs are those sporting the Vegetarian Society tick. Sadly, with only two New Zealand wineries currently approved, the only way of finding out in most cases is to ask the winery directly about what products they've had swimming through their wines.

NEW ZEALAND'S BIG SIX

PERNOD RICARD NEW ZEALAND: French-owned multinational. Labels include Montana, Stoneleigh, Church Road, Five Flax, Camshorn, Jacob's Creek

CONSTELLATION: US-owned multinational. Labels include Nobilo, Drylands, Kim Crawford, Rose Tree Cottage, Selaks, Hardy's, Banrock Station

DELEGAT'S: NZ-owned. Labels include Oyster Bay, Delegat's

VILLA MARIA: NZ family-owned. Labels include Villa Maria, Esk Valley, Vidal

MATUA VALLEY: Australia-owned by multinational Fosters. Labels include Matua Valley, Penfolds, Lindemans, Wolf Blass, Riccadonna

GIESEN: NZ family-owned

Those opting to take a walk on the wild side in their quest for interesting textures and flavours must be prepared to take a chance on the final result. Generally, 'wild ferments' are only used on smaller batches of wine, as this feral approach is regarded as far too risky for large wineries dealing with big volumes.

Some winemakers are also choosing not to filter or fine their wines. While this not only removes potential troublemakers, it can also remove other flavours along with them, which has led those confident of the stability of their wines to dispense with this final clean-up altogether. If you want to try wine that's been made in this way, look for the words 'unfined' and 'unfiltered' that appear predominantly on bottles of premium red.

BIG VERSUS SMALL

Once upon a time, most of the world's wine was made by family-run small holdings, many with no more than a hectare of vines from which to eke their humble living. But with its growing international popularity and profitability, wine has become big business, with many of the wines consumed today the products of massive multinational enterprises.

The big companies have the economies of scale and technology at their fingertips to produce vast volumes of often very respectable wine at competitive prices. But can they be as good as the smaller hands-on operations?

Small wineries have been behind some of the greatest wines, but they've also produced some of the worst, so size isn't everything! While the big companies often use a boutique mentality in the making of their top flagship wines, and are undeniably able to produce wines of excellent quality, the majority of the world's most interesting and distinctive wines are made by the best of the small *vignerons*, whose personal passion and hands-on approach most often guide the wine from grape to bottle.

Fortunately, New Zealand is blessed with a number of big players committed to making quality wine. However, it's with the cheaper and mid-range wines that big companies really excel.

PICKING FAULTS

An understanding of which gremlins can affect wine means that faults are few and far between nowadays. However, there are still a few that slip through even the most stringent quality-control systems which are worth knowing about when tasting wine.

TCA: found in some cork barks, this can impart a dank, mouldy smell and off taste to wine or dull its flavours. While TCA-affected wine used to be quite common, encountering 'corked' wine is now far less likely given the widespread adoption of screwcap and technical corks, as well as improvements to natural corks themselves.

HYDROGEN SULPHIDE: this can form during fermentation and produces eggy and rubbery odours. In small quantities these can be blown off with a few swirls of the glass, but at worst it can leave lingering odours of garlic and sewage. It's become a hot topic due to the fact that the tight seal provided by screwcaps can encourage

FOREIGN OBJECTS

- Cork floating in your wine does not mean it's corked, more likely someone's just been clumsy with the corkscrew.

- Tiny crystals present in white wine are likely to be tartrates. These are perfectly harmless and formed by the crystallisation of a substance found naturally in grapes.

- Cloudiness in older red wines is often just the sediment created as a wine's components fall out with time; generally it just needs to settle to the bottom of the bottle and can be avoided in the glass by decanting.

the fault to develop, although this seems to have been largely remedied through attention to winemaking techniques.

OXIDATION: when excessive oxygen has been absorbed by a wine via a defective closure, this can lead to stale sherry-like aromas in whites and caramelly odours in reds, destroying fruit in wines. Oxidation can make red wines turn brown and darkens whites.

VOLATILE ACIDITY: caused by either acetic acid, a by-product of yeasts in a wine, which produces a vinegary smell and sour taste, or ethyl acetate which is reminiscent of nail polish.

EXCESSIVE SULPHUR DIOXIDE: overuse of this additive can be picked up by its smell, a struck match-like odour that is sometimes sensed as a prickling sensation in the nose and throat. People have varying degrees of sensitivity to sulphur dioxide, which should never cross the line from being an unobtrusive preservative to an overly dominant component of a wine.

BRETTANOMYCES: a naturally occuring yeast that's considered by some as adding complexity and others — especially in the New World — as a nasty spoilage bug due to its barnyard-like character.

1

UNOAKED CHARDONNAY

SUGGESTED WINES

Spring Creek Marlborough Unoaked Chardonnay, $10–15

Tohu Marlborough Unoaked Chardonnay, $15–20

Dolbel Hawke's Bay Unoaked Chardonnay, $20–25

TASTING NOTE: In its pure unoaked form, Chardonnay can show plenty of pure peach and hints of melon over fresh citrus.

2

LIGHTLY OAKED CHARDONNAY

SUGGESTED WINES

Shepherds Ridge Marlborough Chardonnay, $10–15

Sacred Hill Barrel Fermented Hawke's Bay Chardonnay, $15–21

Mahi Marlborough Chardonnay, $21–25

TASTING NOTE: Oak can add toasty spicy notes, hints of which can be found in these examples as well as giving it more weight.

3

OAKY CHARDONNAY

SUGGESTED WINES

Crossroads Hawke's Bay Chardonnay, $20–25
Clearview Beachhead Hawke's Bay Chardonnay, $25–30
Saint Clair Omaka Reserve Marlborough Chardonnay, $30–35

TASTING NOTE: You should still be able to discern a definite peachy fruit character even in this more heavily oaked wine. However, the flavours of the oak are definitely more overt, imparting a range of intense toasty, sweet vanilla and butterscotch notes, often accompanied by a creamy undertone. There should still be a fresh acidity, although this is less evident given the added richness the oak has given to the wine.

4  OAKED SAUVIGNON BLANC

SUGGESTED WINES

Seresin Marama, Marlborough, $35–40

Koru Sauvignon Blanc, Marlborough, $40–45

Cloudy Bay Te Koko, Marlborough, $45–50

TASTING NOTE: While most Sauvignons see no oak, in some reserve examples the winemaker will have used some in varying amounts. This suppresses some of the aromatics but makes the wine feel richer and weightier and can add suggestions of spice when used in moderation, while some examples exhibit quite overt toasty notes. Think back to the Sauvignon you tried in Chapter Two — or crack open another standard Sauvignon — and note how oak has altered the variety's character.

5 ROSÉ

SUGGESTED WINES

Bell Bird Bay Hawkes Bay Rosé, $10–15
Sileni Cellar Selection Hawke's Bay Cabernet Rosé, $15–20
Esk Valley Hawkes Bay Merlot Malbec Rosé, $20–25

TASTING NOTE: Inhale aromas of ripe strawberries and raspberries, which can have a lolly-like character. This is backed up on the palate, where fruit can often combine with notes of cream in some examples or more savoury herbal notes in others. Many have a soupçon of sweetness and much of a good rosé's charm lies in its fresh acidity along with its bright red fruits.

CHAPTER SIX

Taste the Place

'The wonder of wine is that it has the ability to speak of where it comes from, to tell the story of an entire season, in a special, specific place.'

Mike Weersing, Pyramid Valley, Canterbury

Wine has been described as being liquid geography. In the greatest wines, place shines through just as much as the character of the grape variety, sometimes even more so. No other beverage reflects its roots quite as much as wine.

Site specifics

When it comes to making great wines it's all about location, location, location! Some well-appointed spots will make grapes sing, while the wrong situation can strike them dumb, which makes the selection of a vineyard's site incredibly important.

Wine grapes, which come from the *Vitis vinifera* species of vine, can't be grown just anywhere; most of the world's vineyards are found within two bands between the latitudes of 30° and 50° where vines can receive the correct balance of warmth and sunlight they require to ripen, and the coldness they need for dormancy over the winter months. Go north or south of these bands and it's too cold, while in the centre, close to the equator, it's too warm and humid.

Exceptions do occur, such as the floating vineyards of tropical Thailand that manage two vintages a year or the vineyards in nippy northern England. Unless the climate changes, it's doubtful whether fine wine in commercial volumes will ever be made in these extreme regions due to the struggle against considerable odds to harvest quality crops each year.

Favourable climates

Climate has a huge impact on wine, dictating the kind of grapes that can be grown in a particular place and the styles made. Wine regions tend to be on the drier side as grapes are prone to rot in damp and humid conditions, while rain is villain at vintage, because of its ability to dilute the grape's juice and consequently diminish the flavours and intensity of the final wine. That's why most New Zealand vineyards are situated on the east coast rather than the wetter west.

Warm climates tend to be the ones best suited to ripening black grapes, which require more heat and sunshine than white, and are less appropriate for varieties with naturally lower acids, which when grown here can make wines that lack freshness. These climates tend to produce wines with more body, softer acidity, ripe fruit characters and higher alcohol and are home to grape varieties that thrive in the heat. They're also often able to ripen more grapes per vine, which means much of the world's higher volume commercial wines emanate from these hot spots.

Cooler climates come into their own when it comes to grapes requiring a longer growing season to build up flavour. This is the case with many aromatic white varieties and reds such as Pinot Noir, which are unable to develop their essential aromatics and complexity where it's too hot.

Climates are generally considered warm or cool. Warm climates include much of Australia, Spain, southern Italy, southern France, much of South Africa, Chile, and Argentina, while cool climates are somewhat rarer and can be found in places such as Germany, Austria and northern France in the Northern Hemisphere, and Tasmania and New Zealand in the Southern.

Ripening grapes successfully is one of the main challenges in cooler regions. This limits the varieties that can be planted and often requires crop levels to be kept low to ensure complete ripeness — although vines don't tend to carry lots of grapes in cooler climes.

Grape growing in cooler climates may be more difficult, but has its paybacks. Fresher styles of wine with lighter body and crisp acidity, which can also be quite intensely flavoured from the longer time spent ripening on the vine, are often the result. And while sometimes more expensive than their warm-climate counterparts, wines from cooler climes can be among the finest.

Climate can vary within a region, especially when its topography is diverse. Higher altitudes are cooler, which means they tend to be sought out for planting vines in warmer districts, while hillsides facing the sun — southeast and southwest in the northern hemisphere and northeast and northwest in the southern — increase exposure to sunlight, aiding ripening and making them particularly desirable in cooler locations.

Weather with you

Weather has a tremendous effect on wine and is behind the phenomenon known as vintage variation (guaranteed to get the wine buffs burying their noses in vintage charts!).

Reducing the crop size is one of the first things the weather can affect, which can happen through bad weather during flowering, often combined with spring frosts that blast the growing buds. Frost can also strike just before harvest, killing the leaves that are still playing a part in ripening the grapes.

While little can be done at the flowering stage, more action can be taken to fight frost. The dull whirr of helicopter blades is often heard in winegrowing regions during frosty spring nights as helicopters are used to pull down air from inversion layers to stop the colder air reaching the vines on the ground. Protective sprinkler systems, warming the air through burning smudge pots and wind machines are also used to protect the budding vines.

Rain at the wrong time can create havoc in the vineyard. While welcome in winter and beneficial in moderate bursts over the growing season, in the run-up to harvest the sight of grey skies can strike terror into a winegrower's heart. Worse still is the rain that falls during harvest, which can lead to serious dilution and rot.

Temperature variations also impact on style. Some years are warmer, which results in riper wines or even raisined fruit in warmer regions. Cooler years can equate to crisper wines and, in more marginal regions, unripe grapes that can lead to mean, astringent and unpleasantly herbaceous red wines.

In warm, dry climates, growing seasons tend to be quite uniform with not much variation from year to year. In contrast, cooler climes experience far greater fluctuations between vintages in both quality and style, with warmer years often producing the best wines, especially from red varieties such as Cabernet Sauvignon, which can struggle to ripen in a chilly season.

LOUSY TIMES AND GRAFTED VINES

Back in the late nineteenth century, vine growing in Europe almost came to a premature end when a little louse called phylloxera stared nibbling at the roots of the continent's vines leaving a trail of dead plants in its wake.
As phylloxera was only fatal to *Vitis vinifera*, growers experimented by planting species of American vines. While these vines thrived, the problem then became the wine, which didn't taste that flash. An estimated two-thirds of the vineyards of Europe were wiped out before it was discovered that the top parts of the tasty *Vitis vinifera* vines could be grafted onto the resilient roots of the American plants.
Phylloxera is now present in most of the world's winegrowing regions, including New Zealand, making the process of grafting *Vitis vinifera* plants onto phylloxera-resistant rootstock standard practice worldwide today.

THE GOOD, THE BAD AND THE UGLY

Modern viticultural and winemaking techniques have largely made vile vintages a thing of the past. Today, a mediocre vintage is more likely to result in wines that are good rather than great, but will rarely be undrinkable. A good producer can still excel, even in an extreme year, making a trusted name on a label often a far more reliable indication of quality than any vintage date.

However, vintage variation in a fine wine, particularly from a classic cool region such as Bordeaux, is still given great scrutiny, with assessments of the quality of each vintage often determining a wine's price for that year. As these top wines are also made to age, strong vintages are able to evolve over the years into delicious maturity, while lesser ones can have a far shorter lifespan.

While the big commercial brands strive for consistency, variation is an exciting aspect of wine and one of the factors that connect it to its place. Vive la difference!

Back to the soil

Grapevines are contrary creatures. Unlike most crops they do best in difficult terrains where many others fail, while smaller crops, rather than large are the aim of those producing quality wine.

Vines love a bit of stress, and the stoniest, boniest soils will often result in them bearing outstanding fruit. Such an environment forces them to put most of their effort into their fruit rather than foliage and can limit their crop, giving greater concentration.

Soils appear to have a strong influence on a wine's taste and texture: stony soils seem to accentuate aromatics, clays can be reflected in weightier wines, while sandy soils often result in lighter examples. It's even been said that it's possible to taste minerals from the soil in a wine, giving the example of the undeniably minerally wines that often come off rockier ground.

While it's a nice idea, there's no scientific proof. Minerally notes seem to be connected to wines with higher acidities, and could even be a product of certain winemaking techniques. However, what most people agree on, is that hillsides and the free-draining soils, which tend to be the stonier ones, are often the sites behind the greatest wines.

Old vines

It's a widely held view that older vines make consistently better, more concentrated and structured wines, which is why those making wines from older vines will draw attention to it on their labels through the use of terms such as 'Old Vine' or in France, 'Vieille Vignes'. You don't see it mentioned much on New Zealand wine labels, which is hardly surprising given the youth of most of our vineyards. There is currently no legal definition as to what constitutes an 'old vine'. This means you need to approach wine labelled in this way with some caution unless the statement is quantified.

THE VINEYARD CALENDAR

WINTER: vines are dormant and pruned in preparation for the next season.

SPRING: buds swell then burst, leaves and shoots appear, the vine flowers.

SUMMER: shoots proliferate; the fruit develops and starts to ripen, and harvesting starts in warmer climates and for earlier-ripening varieties. In New Zealand the vintage starts as early as February in a warm region like Gisborne and on the other side of the world it generally starts in August.

AUTUMN: this is the main harvest period, with most grapes picked by the end of May in New Zealand and the end of October in much of the Northern Hemisphere. As the weather grows colder, the vines' leaves change colour, then drop.

Terroir-ism

> A wine that says nothing about its place only has one purpose; to get you drunk.
>
> Nigel Greening, Felton Road, Central Otago

Warning: this subject can be explosive! When a special mixture of site, climate and grape combine you get what the French call terroir (pronounced tare-wah), the force behind some of the most mind-blowingly amazing wines. While there's no literal translation of the word, terroir can perhaps best be described as a sense of a wine's 'somewhereness'. It's about the natural environment in which a vine is grown, which includes elements such as the soil, the topography, the climate and the way all these interact.

When there's a synergy between these elements they can imbue wine with a distinctive character that can't be replicated elsewhere and which recurs regardless of variations in vintage, viticulture or winemaking. Drinking 'terroir' wines is like listening to a classic song interpreted by a great singer in an atmospheric venue.

Scientific evidence to support the idea of terroir is scant and there are those that scoff that it's nothing more than fanciful French mythmaking. However, empirical evidence suggests there's definitely something in it.

Many consider humans to be as much a part of terroir as the soil in which the vines grow. A viticulturalist must grow the grapes with meticulous care and the winemaker must carefully craft these into wines that speak of their site. Insensitive handling of the vines, grapes, or wine can ruin a vineyard's potential as easily as a classic song can be mangled by a talentless singer in a karaoke bar.

Human intervention

Left to its own devices, the grapevine would simply snake across the ground until it found a convenient tree or other vertical structure up which to climb. However, human intervention has resulted in the implementation of increasingly sophisticated practices to control and coax the best out of the vines.

While many vines in the traditional wine regions of Europe are of local origin, some have found their way to their current sites via human vectors, and in newer winemaking nations such as New Zealand, people are just starting to match grape varieties to sites with the best climate, aspect and soils to suit their cultivation.

After deciding on the variety, the next major way humans impact on the course of the vine is how the vineyard is set up. They must first decide on how many vines get planted in an allotted space. In France's key quality regions there can be up to 10,000 vines per hectare, while in New Zealand, the norm is around 2500, where row spaces were historically dictated more by the width of the tractor that would pass through them than concerns regarding quality. As higher vine densities encourage the competition which reduces the number of grapes on each vine and can lead to better wines, quality-focused producers in New Zealand are moving towards the French model and planting vines closer together.

BRING ON THE CLONES

This may sound a bit scary, but the clones in question are basically versions of a grape vine variety that have been selected from a single mother vine to enhance certain characteristics: from the quality of the grapes to how they behave in the vineyard. The availability of more super-honed clones and weeding out of lesser ones from modern vineyards has had a major impact on raising wine quality today. While for some grape varieties the type of clone doesn't appear to matter much, for Pinot Noir in particular, having the right ones is more important.

Miles of vines sprawling in all directions would obviously be a nightmare to harvest, hence the neat rows seen in most vineyards. The vines are trained on trellising systems that result in the grapes growing at a practical height for picking; these systems are generally tailored to the type of vine and the vineyard's climatic conditions.

Rather than be left to do their own thing, the vines are tended throughout the year with the ultimate aim of bringing the grapes to perfect ripeness. In countries where it's permitted, the vines can be irrigated (see page 127), as well as fertilisers employed and pests and disease fought off using various treatments.

The amount of grapes each vine bears is another important aspect that can now be managed. As a rule, fewer grapes per vine, equals more concentrated and consequently higher quality final wine. This starts at pruning, which roughly determines the kind of crop a vine will carry and can then be fine-tuned later by shoot-thinning in the spring and by a process called the 'green harvest', where bunches are removed well before reaching maturity, leaving the desired number to ripen on the vine.

When the grapes are ripe and ready for picking, these days it's most often machine harvesters that put in the hard graft, rather than people. These move down the rows gently shaking the vines and collecting the grapes. Hand-picking still occurs in vineyards where slopes or row spacing prevent mechanisation or for premium wines and grape varieties such as Pinot Noir, which require gentler handling or a special selection in the vineyard of the best bunches.

Moving on from those wayward wild vines, growing grapes has become a science: viticulture. Once the domain of the winemaker-grower, grape growing these days is increasingly overseen by a dedicated viticulturalist, especially in larger wine companies. While it's the winemaker who's most frequently seen in the spotlight, collecting wine awards and acting as the face of many wine brands, the viticulturist often has a low public profile that belies the importance of their role. This is easily equal to that of the winemaker as without good grapes, it is impossible for the winemaker to make good wine.

> In wine it's the winemaker that applies the icing, but the viticulturalist that makes the cake.
>
> Bart Arnst, consultant viticulturalist, Marlborough

WATER, WATER EVERYWHERE?

Irrigation has opened up huge tracts of land previously too dry to sustain vines. This includes many of the New World winemaking nations, such as New Zealand, where the majority of vineyards

CLIMATE CHANGE

How about a drop of Pinot Gris from Dunedin? Or maybe a Sauvignon Blanc from Sweden? These wines may not yet exist, but if predictions of global warming prove correct you could be quaffing them in the not-too-distant future as climate change redraws the world's wine map, threatening classic wine styles across the globe. Most grape varieties only perform well within relatively limited climatic bands, so estimates that temperatures may rise between 1°C and 3.5°C by the end of the century could take some of the zing out of styles such as Marlborough Sauvignon. A 2°C hike would put Marlborough's temperatures in the realms of those currently experienced in Auckland, a region not known for its success in making cool-climate aromatics.

However, given the country's location at the coolest end of the vine-growing spectrum and with the vast expanse of sea surrounding it, New Zealand is better placed than many to weather the coming climatic storms. Large warmer land masses such as Australia and continental Europe appear to have things far worse in the years to come, including the possibility that some regions may become too hot for commercial viticulture. Vineyards may have to be moved to higher altitudes and places that were previously too cold to ripen grapes. That glass of wine from Sweden or Dunedin could well become a reality, and may become the new winegrowing hot spots in a warmer world.

THE RISE AND FALL OF ALCOHOL LEVELS

If you've noticed that your glass of wine seems to go to your head more quickly in recent years, it may have less to do with your ability to handle your drink and more with the rising alcohol levels present in many wines today.

Improved viticulture has meant riper grapes and as a consequence alcohol levels have been creeping up. In countries with warmer climates and particularly those with high UV levels, such as New Zealand, grapes often clock up plenty of sugar, and consequently higher alcohol, before their flavours have fully developed.

There's been an international backlash against these high-alcohol wines, which can lack freshness and drinkability. Now a growing number of viticulturalists are striving to ripen grapes at lower sugar levels and picking earlier where possible.

require additions to their water reserves from time to time.

However, in many traditional winemaking areas, irrigation is outlawed. The raison d'être being that irrigation impacts on the quality of the wine, by encouraging large crops and bigger grapes, while stopping the roots of the vines from penetrating deep into the earth to search out water, where they also pick up important minerals.

Used in moderation, irrigation needn't impact on quality, although it's argued that some growers have become overly reliant on it. In this era of droughts there is also increased onus on growers to use water more sparingly, while the long-term viability of regions such as South Australia's Riverland — almost completely reliant on irrigation for its survival — has come under question.

Being green

Modern-day viticulture may embrace state-of-the-art machinery and hi-tech approaches, but over recent years an increasing number of wine folk are choosing to turn back the clock and return to the vine-growing practices of simpler times. While in many ways scientific advances have helped improve the quality of what is coming out of the vineyard, not everyone has been as happy about some of the products that have been going in to them.

Specifically, it's the development and widespread use of chemical fertilisers and pesticides that a number of people in the industry have taken issue with. These 'wonder potions' were initially welcomed by winegrowers when they first came onto the market, but the sorry state of some of the vineyards in traditional winegrowing nations, such as France, after decades of chemical use act as a warning against their overuse.

Existing in soils that chemicals have stripped of their life and nutrients, vines can become dependent on a life-support system of man-made fertilisers, while some pesticides and fungicides can find their way into the finished wine. However, as in all commercial food crops the amount of agrochemical residues in wine is limited by law.

SUSTAINABILITY

Sustainability is the new buzzword hovering above the world's vineyards in this environmentally aware era. New Zealand has got off to a good start in this area as it was one of the first countries to implement a sustainable winegrowing programme, Sustainable Winegrowing New Zealand (SWNZ), as well as the first to boast a carbon neutral winery.

Like most countries, New Zealand has used its fair share of chemicals in the vineyard, but since the SWNZ programme was rolled out commercially in 1997, it has helped wean growers off the excessive spray programmes of the past and into managing their vineyards in a way that requires less chemical intervention. SWNZ hopes to have all the country's grape growers and wineries signed up to it or another similar independently audited sustainability scheme by 2010, with any remaining outside excluded from New Zealand Winegrowers' global marketing programme.

As in many other sustainable winegrowing schemes, SWNZ permits some chemical use. However, for accreditation purposes,

The Sustainable Winegrowing New Zealand logo found on bottles containing wine from accredited vineyards made in accredited wineries

MAKING WINE HOLISTICALLY

Biodynamics is a spiritual and practical philosophy based on the theories of Austrian philosopher Rudolf Steiner. Its main principle is to create a land-holding — whether farm or vineyard — that can become a self-contained, mixed farm providing its own seeds, fertility and feed. The farmer — or vine grower — must develop the right blend of animals, crops and environments to encourage bird and insect life that will result in a 'harmonious and sustainable balance' for each particular holding. Steiner regarded these holdings as part of a wider system of lunar and cosmic rhythms, with which the biodynamic producer works in harmony. Following these lunar rhythms is one of the main areas in which biodynamics and organics differ.

While biodynamics and organics are both concerned with soil health and opposed to synthetic fertilisers or pesticides, biodynamics again differs in the special preparations such as cow horn manure, which are produced through the application of its philosophies.

members must evaluate and explain the need for each spray from an approved section of largely softer products, and use natural and biological alternatives whenever possible.

ORGANIC WINEMAKING

Those wanting to take a natural approach to vine growing one stage further are increasingly opting for growing organically. The organics movement has already gained considerable momentum in other countries, and although less than 2% of New Zealand's vineyards are certified organic, a spurt of interest in the last few years will soon see this percentage increase significantly.

Organic wines are made from grapes that have been grown without the use of synthetic chemicals, which means no chemical fertilisers, pesticides, fungicides or herbicides. Instead, organic producers use entirely natural products with which to feed the soil and fight pests and disease, with a major focus on increasing microbial action within the soil.

To replace what the vines take out of the soil, organic growers make and apply organic composts in their vineyards in place of chemical fertilisers. Pests and diseases are combatted through employing natural products and encouraging predators, such as beneficial insects, to make their home in the vineyard.

Different countries have different organic certification schemes, each of which uses varied criteria. In some this extends beyond the vineyard into the winemaking by limiting the addition of something like sulphites (see page 106). However, any winery wanting to promote themselves as 'organic' must be certified by the local body, which in New Zealand is Bio Gro.

The concept and practice of organics has come a long way in recent years as it is increasingly adopted by quality-focused winemakers who consider organics a vital tool in helping them make better wines.

The Bio Gro logo, used to indicate certified organic wine in New Zealand

BIODYNAMICS

With practices that include burying cow horns filled with manure and hanging yarrow-stuffed stags' bladders from the trees, it is perhaps not surprising that some people regard biodynamics as a bit wacky. These practices may appear to be the antics of a lunatic fringe, but biodynamic methods such as these are being increasingly embraced by some of the most respected names in the wine world, and behind some seriously good wines.

Take a closer look at some of the key biodynamic principles and they start to make more sense, such as the effect the moon has over vines, composed like the ocean is of a high percentage of water. Surveys have also shown that manure dug down in a cow horn contains significantly more bacterial activity than that left in a flowerpot above ground.

Sceptics may need more scientific support, but the proof of biodynamics is in the drinking. There are some great wines being grown biodynamically by people who have a deep connection with their vines. While it could be argued that these producers would have made great wines without using biodynamics, the final result has been enough to convince many key wine critics that biodynamics has played its very valid part.

Pinot Noir is a wine that's often cited as reflecting the character of where it's grown more than any other, with the last three examples in this tasting showing very different regional characters. Kicking off is an edgy cool-climate white, followed by a big, ripe warm-climate red.

1 COOL-CLIMATE GRÜNER VELTLINER

Grüner Veltliners are still relatively rare in New Zealand, although there will be more over the next few years. If you can't track any down, a German or local Riesling can be used as a replacement.

SUGGESTED WINES

Coopers Creek 'The Groover' Gisborne Grüner Veltliner, $20–25
Hiedler Grüner Veltliner Spiegel, Kamptal, Austria, $25–27
Sepp Moser Wolfsgraben Grüner Veltliner, Kremstal, Austria, $27–30

TASTING NOTE: Brisk acidity is at the heart of cool-climate wines. You'll find that its fruit is more at the citrus and stone fruit end of the spectrum, rather than the tropical, maybe accompanied by a twist of lemon zest or even mineral. Look out for Grüner Veltliner's signature note of white pepper.

2

WARM-CLIMATE RED

Head to the Mediterranean or warmer New World climes for the big, bold flavours that typify this style.

SUGGESTED WINES

Carchelo Monastrell/Syrah, Jumilla, Spain, $15–20
Château de Lascaux Côteaux du Languedoc, France, $20–25
La Corte Solyss Negroamaro, Puglia, Italy, $25–30

TASTING NOTE: Warm climates equal ripe fruit and you should almost be able to taste the sun in the sweet sun-baked dark fruit of these wines. Look for lots of colour, rich fruit that could even conjure up compote, prunes or figs, perhaps with a hint of dried Mediterranean herbs and a soft, full body.

3 RED BURGUNDY

SUGGESTED WINES

Joseph Drouhin Côte de Nuits Villages, France, $25–30
Nicolas Potel Cuvée Gerard Potel Bourgogne Pinot Noir, France, $35–40
Anne Gros Bourgogne Pinot Noir, France, $40–45

TASTING NOTE: In the Pinot Noirs of Burgundy, texture is a key component, which should be silky and accompanied by a fresh acidity. Fruit is often quite subtle and in a red berry spectrum, often fused with delicate floral notes, sometimes accompanied by savoury undertones and forest floor.

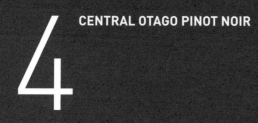

4

CENTRAL OTAGO PINOT NOIR

SUGGESTED WINES

Southern Eclipse Central Otago Pinot Noir, $15–20

Mount Difficulty Roaring Meg, Central Otago Pinot Noir,
  $25–30

Rockburn Central Otago Pinot Noir, $30–45

TASTING NOTE: In contrast with the Burgundy, Central Otago's Pinot Noir is bursting with ripe juicy cherry fruit and spice, often with notes of the thyme that grows wild on the hillsides where the grapes are grown. Supple and plush, Pinot's floral and savoury elements can still be found in the finest examples.

5 WAITAKI PINOT NOIR

Waitaki is making wines in quite small quantities; so if you aren't able to source one from here, select a Pinot Noir from another region.

SUGGESTED WINES

Ostler Waitaki Valley Pinot Noir, $40–45
Valli Waitaki Valley Pinot Noir, $45–55
Waitaki Braids Waitaki Valley Pinot Noir, $55–$60

TASTING NOTE: One of New Zealand's newest regions, Waitaki had people wondering what its terroir would deliver. However, the first Pinots released suggest that its limestone soils and cool climes comparable with those of Burgundy are delivering a Pinot style that straddles Burgundy and New Zealand, with more restrained fruit and what would appear to be the region's signature savoury character.

CHAPTER SEVEN

Regional Round-up — Australasia

'Each area has its own unique set of conditions that lend themselves to a harmony with particular grape varieties. It is the interaction with this "terroir" and the grape and winemaking that makes the challenge and pleasure of our craft.'

Jeff Clarke, Pernod Ricard, New Zealand

NEW ZEALAND:
land of diversity

With its winegrowing regions spread across 1600km and running through two latitudes, New Zealand's wine production can be characterised by its diversity — from the bold red blends and ripe Chardonnays of the north to the subtle Pinot Noirs and edgy aromatic whites of the south.

Synergies between certain districts and grape varieties have already been discovered — such as the magic between Marlborough and Sauvignon Blanc — and more are probably yet to come given the youth of New Zealand's wine industry. A heady mix of experimentation and excitement is fermenting in the established regions, taking their wines to higher quality levels, while the potential of new sub-regions is just starting to be explored.

MARLBOROUGH: Sauvignon country

When Marlborough Sauvignon Blanc exploded onto the world wine scene in a pungent riot of lime, passionfruit and gooseberry, no one had tasted anything quite like it. This wasn't the restrained style wine experts knew from the Loire; it was something completely different.

First planted in the region in 1975, Marlborough's unique style of Sauvignon has driven the expansion of what has become the country's largest winegrowing region, and played a key part in the success of the country's wine industry as a whole.

Most Marlborough Sauvignons are made from a blend of grapes from across the region. However, as the region has expanded into new sub-regions, different expressions of the classic Marlborough style are starting to emerge. In its Wairau Valley heartland it makes powerful pungent Sauvignons bursting with ripe passionfruit, while the slightly cooler southern valleys are producing wines with more subtle aromatics and greater texture. Even further south on the other side of the Wither Hills, the Awatere Valley is home to a distinctively racy greener style, often with notes of tomato stalk and mineral.

Sauvignon Blanc still reigns supreme in the region, accounting for over two-thirds of Marlborough's annual wine production, but co-exists with many other varieties. It is the location of the country's highest percentage of Pinot Noir plantings which is now its second most important grape. Marlborough's bright plummy Pinots have been acquiring more gravitas as its vines have increasingly come to be sited in the Southern and Awatere valleys best suited to the variety.

Marlborough also produces crisp Chardonnays and is now home to a host of aromatics that share the freshness and vibrancy of the region's star performer.

KEY GRAPE VARIETIES: SAUVIGNON BLANC, PINOT NOIR, CHARDONNAY, AROMATIC WHITES

HAWKE'S BAY: master of many

Hawke's Bay has established itself as one of New Zealand's most important wine regions, not least for doing a lot of things very well. Known for some of the country's finest Chardonnays, this long-standing region is one of the few able to ripen red varieties such as Merlot and Cabernet Sauvignon, which form the basis of the region's increasingly fine and darkly fruited Bordeaux blends.

Over recent years excitement has mounted over the local Syrah, a new grape to the region that's making juicy black pepper-infused examples comparable to those from the variety's heartland of the northern Rhône. Viognier, too, is also starting to take off, with vibrantly aromatic stand-alone examples as well as being present in tiny proportions in some of the region's Syrahs.

Hawke's Bay is also a major producer of Sauvignon Blanc, but as the local climate is warmer than Marlborough, they are weightier and more tropical, often benefiting from some barrel-fermented components which add texture and spice that suit the richer Hawke's Bay style.

KEY GRAPE VARIETIES: CHARDONNAY, MERLOT, BORDEAUX BLENDS, SAUVIGNON BLANC, SYRAH, PINOT GRIS, VIOGNIER

GISBORNE: beyond the cask

Vying with Hawke's Bay to be the country's Chardonnay capital, Gisborne is also trying to shrug off its image as cask wine country. While much of its wine has ended up as Château Cardboard or in the anonymous east coast multi-regional blends put together by the big wine companies, over recent years a rising number of small growers, new boutique wineries and large wine companies have released their own Gisborne-specific labels, proving that these east coast players can make some really exciting wines.

Whites are Gisborne's real strength; on top of its ripe tropically fruited Chardonnays the region is currently building a reputation for white aromatics that thrive in its warmer climes, such as Gewürztraminer and Viognier.

KEY GRAPE VARIETIES: CHARDONNAY, PINOT GRIS, MERLOT, GEWÜRZTRAMINER, VIOGNIER

CENTRAL OTAGO: treasures from the gold country

Over a century ago it was miners hoping to strike gold who flocked to the dry hills of Central Otago. In the last decade it's been winemakers who have come prospecting here, looking to find new gold in the form of the region's distinctive Pinot Noirs.

With their vibrant cherry fruit and spice, Central's Pinots have attracted major interest and accolades from across the world. They don't come cheap, given the physical impossibility of mechanising many Central vineyards and the incredibly low crops that come with growing vines in the world's most southerly winegrowing region. However, greater volumes in recent years as new vineyards come on stream have meant more affordable examples becoming available.

Pinot Noir dominates Central Otago, covering over three-quarters of its vineyard area. However, it's worth checking out some of Central's other highlights including its citrusy Rieslings and crisp minerally style of Pinot Gris.

KEY GRAPE VARIETIES: PINOT NOIR, PINOT GRIS, CHARDONNAY, RIESLING

WAIPARA AND CANTERBURY: limestone legacy

Limestone is widely credited as being the dirt behind the distinctive wines from France's Burgundy region. Spread liberally across the north and northwest facing slopes of Waipara and in outcrops elsewhere in Canterbury, this and the region's relatively cool climate, has acted as a magnet to winemakers, especially in recent years when many newcomers have rocked up for a piece of Waipara's action in particular.

Just as Pinot Noir is Burgundy's limestone-loving red grape, it's Waipara's main red, too. Often with darker denser fruit than those of Marlborough, Waipara Pinots from the region's longest-established winegrowers especially have proved they can make them to compete with the best in the land.

Then there is the region's minerally and lime 'cordial'-infused Riesling, often made in a slightly sweeter style, that has become Waipara's signature white variety. Its Pinot Gris, which combines freshness with concentration, has also been showing real promise.

On the cooler more frost-prone plains of the wider Canterbury district, some players may have been lost to warmer regions, but those who are left are largely focused on running quality operations. Their crisp light Rieslings in particular illustrate that grape growing here is still a worthwhile endeavour for those prepared to rise to its challenges. Warmer sites around Banks Peninsula have also had considerable success with Pinot Noir and increasingly Pinot Gris.

KEY GRAPE VARIETIES: PINOT NOIR, RIESLING, PINOT GRIS, SAUVIGNON BLANC, CHARDONNAY

MARTINBOROUGH/WAIRARAPA: Pinot pioneers

'Small is beautiful' could well be Martinborough's mantra. Not only does it apply to the geographical proportions of the Wairarapa's most famous wine region, but also to its predominantly boutique players and the quantity of wines they produce.

With Pinot Noir vineyards dating back to the early 1980s, Martinborough has New Zealand's longest track record with the variety; it's home to some of the widely acknowledged 'greats' and the source of some of the most structured, concentrated and long-lived examples.

While Pinot accounts for the highest percentage of its production, Martinborough also makes some zesty and herbaceous Sauvignon, crisp minerally Riesling, as well as some excellent examples of Chardonnay, Gewürztraminer and Pinot Gris.

Winegrowing has now spread north into the wider Wairarapa and while this sub-region is slightly cooler, its wines follow similar stylistic lines to those of Martinborough, with Pinot Noir, Sauvignon and Chardonnay being its major varieties.

KEY GRAPE VARIETIES: PINOT NOIR, SAUVIGNON BLANC, RIESLING, CHARDONNAY

NELSON: boutique and Bohemian

While often overshadowed by its powerhouse of a neighbour, the small arty region of Nelson, to the west of Marlborough, is starting to craft its own identity through its diverse assortment of wines.

It's a burgeoning boutique winery scene of mostly family-owned establishments, a number of which are producing wines which can excel in terms of value and, increasingly, quality with the region already boasting some of the country's top Pinot Noirs and Chardonnays. It's also building an increasing following for its softer-style Sauvignon, and other fresh and vibrant aromatic white varieties.

KEY GRAPE VARIETIES: SAUVIGNON BLANC, PINOT NOIR, CHARDONNAY, AROMATIC WHITES

NORTHLAND AND AUCKLAND: rising to the challenge

With its wet and humid climate, this part of the country can pose something of a challenge when it comes to growing quality grapes. But despite the relatively small quantities of wine being made — some of which is decidedly mediocre — there are some exceptional wines to be found.

In Northland, Syrah is starting to show promise. Further south, Bordeaux blends have been the staple of Matakana, and the region is also starting to do some good things with Chardonnay and Pinot Gris.

Waiheke Island's winegrowers claim their climate offers more favourable conditions for winegrowing than elsewhere in the greater Auckland region, with a longer growing season to give the black grapes that dominate its vineyards a greater chance of ripening. While some of its Bordeaux blends can be a touch herbaceous, the best are very good indeed, if a little pricey. Syrah is also starting to take off, and among the white varieties, soft and full-bodied Chardonnay is its strongest player.

Elsewhere, individual wineries are triumphing against adverse climatic conditions: some of the country's greatest Chardonnays can be found in Kumeu while elegant Bordeaux blends triumph in Clevedon.

KEY GRAPE VARIETIES: CHARDONNAY, MERLOT, CABERNET SAUVIGNON, SYRAH

WAIKATO AND BAY OF PLENTY: grapes from other sources

It was in the small northern Waikato town of Te Kauwhata that one of the founding fathers of the New Zealand wine industry, Romeo Bragato, set up his first viticultural research centre at the start of the 1900s. Given that the region's biggest names no longer source much of their grapes from this warm, humid district, its significance as a wine region largely rests on Bragato's efforts. However, those making wines in the country's smallest established wine region are producing soft, fleshy whites from Chardonnay and Sauvignon Blanc, and spicy Bordeaux blends.

KEY GRAPE VARIETIES: CHARDONNAY, CABERNET SAUVIGNON, SAUVIGNON BLANC, MERLOT

WAITAKI VALLEY: new vines on the block

The limestone slopes of this diminutive new and ultra-cool-climate wine region northwest of Oamaru in the South Island have attracted the interest and investment of a number of the country's leading winemakers. While they may only have a handful of vintages behind them, the initial releases of Pinot Noir, Riesling and Pinot Gris suggest it's a region to watch.

KEY GRAPE VARIETIES: PINOT NOIR, RIESLING, PINOT GRIS

AUSTRALIA: red hot

Australia is the master of the multi-regional blend, which involves grapes grown thousands of kilometres apart combined in a massive mélange and then largely sold as the product of 'South Eastern Australia'.

Many of these wines rely on fruit from arid but irrigated inland regions such as South Australia's Riverland, which produces soft, ripe, fruity and affordable everyday quaffers with no real stamp of place. However, get into the country's specific wine regions and you'll encounter the real character of Australian wine.

Wines from this big hot country have historically been beefy, full-bodied fare. However, with the exploitation of cooler sites come lighter fresher styles, leading to far greater diversity over the last decade.

BAROSSA: old vines and big wines

Well known for its blockbusting Shiraz, chock-full of plush dark fruit, seasoned with cedary oak and a liberal dash of spice, the Barossa Valley in South Australia boasts a quantity of gnarled old vines that are responsible for some of its best wines. Dating back in some cases to 1855 — which makes them among the world's oldest vines — these venerable vines are still yielding tiny quantities of amazingly rich and concentrated fruit.

Styles tend to be more on the robust side, given the Barossa's warm climate, with grapes such as Grenache, Cabernet Sauvignon and Mataro (Mourvèdre) making big red wines, which are complemented by the region's rich Chardonnays and ripe but lemony Sémillons.

Higher in the hills, and consequently cooler, is the Eden Valley. Here, they've been able to make fresher styles of Shiraz and limey-tasting Rieslings that number among some of the country's best.

KEY GRAPE VARIETIES: SHIRAZ, CABERNET SAUVIGNON, CHARDONNAY, SÉMILLON, GRENACHE

CLARE VALLEY: Riesling riddle

Something of an enigma because of its location in hot inland South Australia, the Clare Valley surprisingly produces some of the country's best cool-climate loving Riesling, alongside substantial Shirazes and big burly Cabernets.

The secret is in its altitude, which provides this arid region with the cool nights and breezes that are necessary to produce its famous steely dry Rieslings. The hillsides also boast a number of different aspects and soils creating mesoclimates that result in a surprising array of styles.

KEY GRAPE VARIETIES: RIESLING, SHIRAZ, CABERNET SAUVIGNON

COONAWARRA: terra rossa terrain

Soil has arguably become more of a focal point in South Australia's Coonawarra than anywhere else in Australia. The dirt in question is the red terra rossa soil, thought to be behind the intense flavours and structure of the region's wines. When official boundaries were drawn up earlier this decade in order to identify the vineyards that feature this distinctive soil, a number of wineries that had for years labelled themselves as from Coonawarra were excluded, resulting in some fierce territorial battles.

With a climate that's warm by New Zealand standards and therefore able to reliably ripen the Cabernet Sauvignon that is the undisputed King of Coonawarra, it's still one of Australia's cooler regions, producing an elegant style of Cabernet that's known for its suppleness and concentration, blackcurrent fruit and minty edge.

KEY GRAPE VARIETIES: CABERNET SAUVIGNON, SHIRAZ, CHARDONNAY

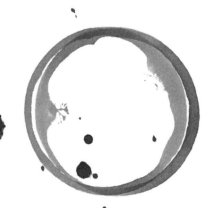

YARRA VALLEY: cool customer

Close to the city of Melbourne, the Yarra Valley is arguably Australia's mainland cool-climate capital. While much of Australia is too sweltering for the likes of heat-sensitive Pinot Noir, here they make a soft and elegant style, along with fresher Chardonnay, some of the country's top sparkling wines, a lighter more restrained Rhône-like style of Syrah and even some botrytised dessert wines.

Although its grape-growing history dates back to the mid-1800s, it was largely abandoned until the renaissance of the 1960s that started to gather serious momentum in the 1980s and which continues into the twenty-first century as the current demand for cooler climate styles grows.

KEY GRAPE VARIETIES: CHARDONNAY, PINOT NOIR, CABERNET SAUVIGNON, SHIRAZ

TASMANIA: devilishly good

According to climate data, the winegrowing regions of this island south of Melbourne have comparable conditions to those of Marlborough and Martinborough. So, unsurprisingly, in Australia's coolest region, you'll see similar grapes and styles to those found in New Zealand, which is why not much of it is imported here. But if you do get the chance, it's well worth seeking out some of Tasmania's fantastic fizz, delicate Chardonnay and attractive aromatics such as Riesling, Pinot Gris and Sauvignon Blanc. It is also starting to make some of the country's most impressive Pinot Noirs.

KEY GRAPE VARIETIES: PINOT NOIR, CHARDONNAY, SAUVIGNON BLANC, RIESLING

MARGARET RIVER: way out west

Margaret River's Bordeaux-like climate, with its maritime influence and relatively cool average temperatures, led to the establishment of this small but prestigious region in Western Australia. And it was Bordeaux's great grape Cabernet Sauvignon, which makes ripe but elegant examples here, upon which it founded its reputation.

Along with Cabernet Sauvignon, Merlot is increasing in popularity, while Margaret River has also adopted Bordeaux's other classic combo of Sauvignon Blanc and Sémillon, making fresh grassy examples, often with plenty of concentration. Straying from Bordeaux's varietal mix, it also makes some outstanding Chardonnays, which although ripe and viscous are balanced by their crisp cool-climate acidity.

KEY GRAPE VARIETIES: CABERNET SAUVIGNON, CHARDONNAY, SAUVIGNON BLANC, SÉMILLON, SHIRAZ, MERLOT

HUNTER VALLEY: difficult but distinctive

Given its hot and humid climate, fertile soils, and the ever-present threat of rain at vintage, the Hunter Valley seems an unlikely spot for growing good grapes. Despite the odds, it's produced wines that have helped put Australia on the world's wine map.

Hunter Sémillon is one of the world's truly unique styles of wine — light, tight and lemony in its youth, blossoming with age into a honeyed, toasty and buttery beauty, which can develop and last for decades.

In this fruit-driven age, the valley's earthy, savoury and leathery Shirazes are not quite in tune with current tastes, despite losing their 'sweaty saddle' note, which is now acknowledged to be a winemaking fault rather than a regional characteristic. However, the Hunter is also producing a new wave of fruitier wines, which include soft peachy Chardonnay and fresh fruity Verdelho.

KEY GRAPE VARIETIES: CHARDONNAY, SHIRAZ, SÉMILLON, VERDELHO

OUTER REACHES

Australia is peppered with small regions that produce a variety of exciting wines, particularly the cooler locations. One of note is South Australia's Adelaide Hills from which some of the country's most elegant Chardonnay and serious Sauvignon has emanated in recent years, as well some great sparklers and Pinot Noir.

Further south, the Limestone Coast — with its vineyards situated around the districts of Padthaway, Coonawarra, Wrattonbully, Robe and Mt Benson — has recently been the site of increased vineyard planting by those looking to make premium wines in its cooler climate and limestone soils, and is producing an expanding array of interesting wines.

Another chillier region of note is the Mornington Peninsula southeast of Melbourne where they make light, crisp and intense Pinot Noir, Chardonnay and Riesling.

While tastes may be moving towards cooler climate wines, back in South Australia McLaren Vale is still worth a mention as one of the country's prime warmer regions. Undeniably hot, it's close to the Barossa in terms of location and style, producing strapping Shiraz, gutsy Grenache and dense dark Cabernet, as well as some commendable Chardonnay.

1 MARLBOROUGH SAUVIGNON BLANC

SUGGESTED WINES

Mount Riley Marlborough Sauvignon Blanc, $15–20

Astrolabe Marlborough Sauvignon Blanc, $20–25

Montant 'B' Brancott Marlborough Sauvignon Blanc, $25–35

TASTING NOTE: With its pungent nose of fresh green herbs, gooseberries and passion fruit, Marlborough Sauvignon is often one of the first wines people are able to spot 'blind'. These aromas lead through to the palate, where they're joined by zippy lemons and limes and maybe a hint of mineral.

2 MARTINBOROUGH PINOT NOIR

SUGGESTED WINES

Te Hera Kiritea Martinborough Pinot Noir, $15–20

Julicher 99 Rows Martinborough Pinot Noir, $25–30

Escarpment Martinborough Pinot Noir, $30–45

TASTING NOTE: Martinborough's Pinot Noirs tend to be more dense and meaty than those made elsewhere in the country. These examples can have a slightly fuller body and attractive savoury nuances, although styles can vary between producers.

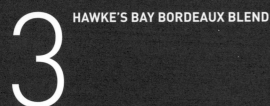

3

HAWKE'S BAY BORDEAUX BLEND

SUGGESTED WINES

Beach House Hawke's Bay Cabernet Merlot, $15–20

Alluviale Hawke's Bay Merlot Cabernet, $20–25

Unison Hawke's Bay Red, $25–30

TASTING NOTE: Making some of the fullest-bodied reds, the best from the Bay can have a wonderful structure, with ripe but evident tannins and fresh acidity supporting elegant dark berry fruit and often notes of cedar from barrel ageing.

4

CLARE VALLEY RIESLING

SUGGESTED WINES

Tim Gramp Clare Valley Watervale Riesling, Australia, $20–25
Pikes Clare Valley Traditionale Dry Riesling, Australia, $25–30
Grosset Clare Valley Watervale Riesling, Australia, $30–40

TASTING NOTE: After sniffing out its citrusy nose, in the first sip you should be struck by the crunchy core of lime and green apple in this variety, often accompanied by notes of mineral, with toasty and honeyed nuances present in those from older vintages.

5 BAROSSA SHIRAZ

SUGGESTED WINES

Manara Rock Barossa Shiraz, Australia, $10–15

Thorn-Clarke Sandpiper Barossa Shiraz, Australia, $15–20

Elderton Barossa Shiraz, Australia, $20–30

TASTING NOTE: Plums, spice and cedary oak emanating from the glass should be echoed on the palate of this big-bodied wine. Boasting lots of ripe dark fruit, this wine's tannins and acidity are on the softer side.

6 MARGARET RIVER CABERNET/BLEND

SUGGESTED WINES

Ringbolt Margaret River Cabernet Sauvignon, Australia,
  $15–21

Sandalford Margaret River Estate Reserve Cabernet Sauvignon,
  Australia, $21–30

Cape Mentelle 'Trinders' Margaret River Cabernet Merlot,
  Australia, $30–40

TASTING NOTE: Margaret River makes a particulary elegant
style of Cabernet/Cabernet blends in which you should sense
a lovely juicy acidity driving through a palate packed with
concentrated classic blackcurrant fruit. Their ripe dark fruit
is regularly underpinned by a savoury and sometimes herbal
character and understated notes of coffee bean-like oak.

CHAPTER EIGHT

Further Afield

'It is not just a bottle of wine, but the whole story
that goes with it. That is the exiting part!'

Jean-Christophe Poizat, Maison Vauron, Auckland

There are some who mistakenly regard it as an act of treason to drink wines from elsewhere in the world. Our homegrown product may never have been better, but such loyalty means missing out on a multitude of tastes and textures specific to the many different places in which wine grapes are grown and prevents us from putting our own wines in an international context.

We become better judges of the character and quality of our local wines once we've benchmarked them against classic examples, such as Sauvignon Blanc from the Loire, Pinot Noir from Burgundy and Riesling from Germany, and seen how varieties from other New World countries shape up against our own, such as the Sauvignon Blancs of Chile and South Africa.

Venturing into European wines can be daunting. There's the issue of alien grape varieties or labels that make no mention of any variety at all, the hard-to-pronounce names and the unfamiliar producers. Assistance from a knowledgeable wine merchant can be invaluable in overcoming these hurdles.

Many European wines also need to be approached from a slightly different angle than those of the New World. Rather than fruit being to the fore, the focus of European wines tends to be on texture; this is because so many of them have been made specifically to go with food, which can really bring them to life.

NEW WORLD VERSUS OLD

As touched on earlier, the world's winegrowing nations are often divided into the Old and New World. In the former, some regions have had centuries, if not thousands of years, to find the perfect union of place, grape and style, which have often become enshrined in laws that dictate which grapes may be grown where and which style/s can be made, with some even stipulating how the grapes must be grown and the resulting wines made. While this approach has served to protect and preserve traditional combinations, it can limit experimentation.

In contrast, the approach among New World nations is far more flexible, as many of them are just starting to explore their wine regions and are still discovering the grapes and styles that will work for them. Both approaches have their merits and disadvantages.

In recent years there has been plenty of cross-pollination between the two winemaking worlds. Winemakers from the Old World continue to act as consultants to New World wineries, even establishing their own vineyards to take advantage of the freedom to try out their home varieties in different soils and situations.

Then there are the many New World winemakers who often work a number of vintages in Europe to learn and benefit from the centuries of experience on offer there. Some have become Flying Winemakers, consulting in long-established regions and acting as a vector for the transfer of modern ideas and expertise to traditional winegrowing nations.

OLD WORLD WONDERS

FRANCE:
Gallic greats

French wines may account for just a petite proportion of the wines we see in New Zealand, but their importance belies our modest imports. With a resonance that reverberates across vineyards around the globe, including ours where French grapes account for much of what's grown, their classic styles continue to inspire winemakers worldwide.

However, it's easy to feel overwhelmed by France's complex appellation system that's based on geographical names rather than grape varieties. It's worth persevering, though, as when it comes to the sheer scope and the quality of its greatest wines, France is hard to beat.

BORDEAUX: châteaux lands

It's the imposing châteaux and their lofty wines that spring to mind when one thinks of Bordeaux. However, while it produces some of the most highly prized and priced wines in the world as Europe's largest quality-wine region it's also the supplier of vast volumes of everyday examples that you don't have to be on the Rich List to buy.

Best known for its great red blends from the Médoc — situated on the gravelly left bank of the Gironde River that winds through the heart of the region — these tend to be Cabernet Sauvignon dominant. On the limestone and clays of its right bank in appellations such as Pomerol and St Émilion, it's Merlot, the region's most widely planted variety, that has more of a monopoly, often with a soupçon of Cabernet Franc added to its blends.

But Bordeaux is not just about reds, it's also the source of Sauvignon Blanc-Sémillon blends that range from the simple and grassy to complex and minerally, as well as some lusciously sweet noble-rot affected wines from appellations such as Sauternes and Barsac.

KEY GRAPE VARIETIES: MERLOT, CABERNET SAUVIGNON, CABERNET FRANC, SAUVIGNON BLANC, SÉMILLON

BURGUNDY: multi-layered complexity

While Bordeaux and Burgundy compete with each other as producers of some of France's finest wines, Burgundy is on a far smaller scale than Bordeaux in terms of overall size and volume of wine produced, right down to its patchwork of tiny plots that can sometimes comprise just a few rows of vines.

Its cool hillsides are home to some of the world's greatest Pinot Noirs, made in a smorgasbord of styles from the soft and fragrant Chambolle-Musigny to the dense richness of the best Gevrey-Chambertin, with its undulating landscape producing marked variation in wines often within tiny areas. Only in the Beaujolais sub-region will you encounter any other kind of black grape, where Gamay produces simpler light and juicy wines.

In the benchmark Chardonnay of the region, terroir also makes a special mark. In its most northerly sub-region of Chablis, Chardonnays are minerally and austere, gaining weight through the Côte d'Or, the source of prime examples such as the ripe and nutty Meursault and powerfully poised Puligny-Montrachet. Head further south and the styles become softer and simpler in the Côte Chalonnaise and Côte Mâconnais, but which can offer good value at far lower prices in comparison to their northern neighbours.

KEY GRAPE VARIETIES: CHARDONNAY, PINOT NOIR, GAMAY (IN BEAUJOLAIS)

CHAMPAGNE: the finest fizz

For the skinny on France's finest sparkling region, turn back to page 85.

KEY GRAPE VARIETIES: CHARDONNAY, PINOT NOIR, PINOT MEUNIER

THE LOIRE VALLEY: seminal Sauvignons

If you want to try a seminal Sauvignon Blanc, then look to the Loire, home to the grapefruity fresh and minerally Sancerre, the flinty smoky specimens of Pouilly Fumé (fumé means smoke in French) or the simpler but zesty and herbaceous Touraine Sauvignon Blancs.

However, the Loire is more than a one-trick pony, as it also makes racy Chenin Blanc in styles from dry to sparkling to very sweet in the appellation of Vouvray: minerally and dry in Savennières and luscious in the Côteaux du Layon.

Then there are its light and aromatic reds made from Cabernet Franc in the likes of Chinon, Bourgueil and Saumur-Champigny, plus a handful of Pinot Noirs, rosés in Anjou and fresh citrusy seaspray-like Muscadets from closer to the coast.

KEY GRAPE VARIETIES: SAUVIGNON BLANC, CHENIN BLANC, MUSCADET, CABERNET FRANC, PINOT NOIR

GETTING TO KNOW THE CRU

Cru is the French term for vineyard. Literally meaning 'growth', this word is appended to the terms 'Grand' and 'Premier' on wines from Bordeaux and Burgundy where they are part of their quality classification system.

In Bordeaux the top wines of its Médoc region have been ranked from first to fifth growths, with the top category of first growths (also known as Premiers Crus) featuring five of the world's most esteemed and expensive labels. Some other Bordeaux sub-regions, such as St Émilion, have a slightly different system with just the two categories of first and second growth for their finest estates. This is also true of Sauternes, which has the extra-special accolade of 'First Great Growth' awarded only to Château d'Yquem.

Cru Bourgeois is the category beneath the classed growths and above generic Bordeaux. A furore followed its revision in 2003, which saw only 247 out of 490 châteaux receive cru bourgeois status, with a number of excluded properties taking the decision to the courts. It was consequently scrapped, then reinstated in 2009.

To make things even more confusing, Burgundy's system calls its highest ranking wines Grand Cru, with Premier Cru beneath it. These relate to the two grades of individual vineyard sites and not single estates. Then you come to Chablis, where its single Grand Cru is spread over several plots of land!

ALSACE: essentially aromatic

Despite various changes of rule during its history, which have involved this northeastern region switching between being part of Germany and France, it's consistently been the producer of some of the world's most enthralling aromatic whites.

Marked by their purity and intensity, these include its steely dry Riesling, rich and spicy Tokay-Pinot Gris (the local name for Pinot Gris), powerful and perfumed Gewürztraminer, sweet Vendage Tardive (Late Harvest) wines and even sweeter botrytis-affected Sélection de Grains Nobles (Selection of Noble Grapes).

KEY GRAPE VARIETIES: RIESLING, GEWÜRZTRAMINER, PINOT GRIS, PINOT NOIR, MUSCAT, PINOT BLANC

THE RHÔNE VALLEY: Que Syrah Syrah

Split into two distinct regions, north and south, the former's wines are largely focused on the exotically aromatic, peppery spiced and juicily red fruited wines made from the only red grape grown here, Syrah. This variety graces the steep slopes of its Côte Rôtie and Hermitage Hill, as well as the lesser but worthy appellations of Crozes-Hermitage, Cornas and St Joseph. There is also a tiny amount of white grapes grown here. The most important is Viognier, from which some of the variety's most refined stand-alone wines are made in Condrieu, which also finds its way in small quantities into the red Côte Rôtie.

In the more expansive south, Syrah is joined in the dominant rich spicy red blends, from the likes of the Côtes du Rhône,

Gigondas and Châteauneuf-du-Pape, by a host of other grapes including Grenache and Mourvèdre.

A few southern white wines are also found here, made from lesser-known varieties such as Roussane, Clairette and Grenache Blanc, but are rarely seen for sale in New Zealand.

KEY GRAPE VARIETIES: SYRAH, VIOGNIER, MARSANNE, ROUSSANNE, GRENACHE, MOURVÈDRE

SOUTHERN FRANCE: Mediterranean mentality

While boasting its own selection of specific appellations, much of southern France is Vin de Pays country (defined as 'country wine', the category below appellation contrôlée). This means fewer restrictions on what winemakers are permitted to do, allowing for the planting of a wider range of varieties.

Once mainly known as a purveyor of vast quantities of plonk, recent investment has changed this. Inspired by the freedom offered outside the confines of appellation contrôlée and with the application of modern winemaking, its reputation has been transformed into one for innovation and as a maker of attractive fruit-filled wines.

Stylistically the rich ripe and soft wines of the south's large Languedoc-Roussillon region can be reminiscent of many in Australia; understandable given their comparably hot dry climates.

Syrah is a strong variety here, along with other Rhône reds, such as Grenache, as well as increasing amounts of Cabernet

Sauvignon and Merlot. White wine is of less importance to the region, although it can make some lovely rich Chardonnay and Viognier.

Outside its Vin de Pays, southern appellations include Provence with its well-known rosés, the big dark Mourvèdre-based wines of Bandol, and sturdy reds of Minervois and Corbières.

In the southwest, closer to Bordeaux, the chewy Tannats of Madiran and inky Malbecs of Cahors are also worth a mention.

KEY GRAPE VARIETIES: SYRAH, GRENACHE, CHARDONNAY, MOURVÈDRE, CARIGNAN, CINSAUT, CABERNET SAUVIGNON, MERLOT, VIOGNIER, MARSANNE, ROUSSANNE

ITALY:
la dolce vino

With 500 different appellations, thousands of wineries — most of which are very small — a million growers and a history of variable quality, the process of exploring Italian wines has been something of a white-knuckle ride. However, with huge improvements in quality, it's a trip definitely worth taking through its range of breathtaking top wines to increasingly well made and fruity everyday examples.

From Aleatico to Zibibbo, Italy boasts an amazing array of indigenous grapes that provide interesting alternatives to the international staples. It also has many different regions, from misty Piedmont in the north to scorching Sicily in the south providing a truly varied range of styles.

The cool northwestern region of Piedmont is famous for its lighter bodied Barolo and Barbaresco wines that offer a fascinating fusion of high tannin and acid under the bewitching Nebbiolo grape's trademark aromatics of tar and roses.

Travel east to Verona and you're in the land of Soave and Valpolicella. While each of these wines once could regularly disappoint, happily both have significantly improved in recent years. In the past viewed largely as a characterless quaffing wine, Soave, for example, now more frequently expresses the wine's positives of pure lemony fruit and almondy undertones. The soft cherry-fruited Valpolicella is also getting into gear, and if you're looking for one with more grunt, try the 'ripasso' style. This has often gained richness from being fermented on the skins of Valpolicella's other great rich wine, the powerful dry Amarone that's made from dried grapes along with Valpolicella's sweet style, Recioto.

Further down the country, Tuscany is home to Chianti, made predominantly from one of Italy's most important grapes, Sangiovese. With the planting of better quality vines has come higher quality wines, which exhibit greater intensity, while denser and supple Sangiovese often comes from Brunello di Montalcino and Vino Nobile di Montepulciano. In Tuscany, Montepulciano is a place, not a grape, unlike in Montepulciano d'Abruzzo, where it's a variety that can produce dark chocolatey wines in the more southerly region of Abruzzo.

Down in the heel of Italy's boot, Puglia is kicking up plenty of excitement with the native Primitivo and Negroamaro varieties. While the sun-drenched south was once the source of blending material to bump up weaker bulk wines made elsewhere, the region of Puglia and the island of Sicily — with its own indigenous Nero d'Avola grape — are now making a name for themselves as producers of rich, ripe, darkly fruited, full-bodied and competitively priced wines.

KEY GRAPE VARIETIES: SANGIOVESE, BARBERA, NEBBIOLO, NEGROAMARO, NERO D'AVOLA, PRIMITIVO, MONTEPULCIANO, DOLCETTO, CORVINA, CABERNET SAUVIGNON, MERLOT, PINOT GRIGIO, CHARDONNAY, MOSCATO, GARGANEGA, TREBBIANO

SPAIN:
a new revolution

For many people, Spain is still associated with rough reds or Rioja. However, over recent years Spain's wine styles and regions have undergone something of a revolution, resulting in its wines becoming fresher and more fruit-driven, with less excessive ageing in oak. A new generation of skilled and well-travelled winemakers has helped catapult the country to the forefront of modern European winemaking, making it one of the most New World-like of the Old World winemaking nations.

While 'international' varieties such as Cabernet Sauvignon, are now grown in regions such as Navarra, Spain has also guarded its own treasures in its indigenous grape varieties and amazing old vines, whose grapes can even enrich more modest bottles.

Tempranillo is Spain's main indigenous grape variety, advancing across vineyards throughout the country under various names, and often complemented by Mediterranean varieties such as Garnacha (Grenache) and Monastrell (Mourvèdre).

In Spain's most famous region of Rioja, Tempranillo makes an array of styles from light strawberry-fruited affairs to ones with lashings of sweet oak and some increasingly refined and elegant examples. Head west to another of the country's major quality wine regions, Ribera del Duero, and you'll find it a more muscular and brooding beast.

In the environs of Rioja, in the great-value wines of the lesser-known regions of Campo de Borja, Cariñena and Calatayud, Tempranillo is joined by Garnacha. It also makes decent everyday examples in Spain's arid dry heart La Mancha and in the districts of Valdepeñas and Valencia, as well as with Monastrell in Murcia.

It's Garnacha that's behind the great and intense wines of Spain's other top-quality region, Priorat. While in the up-and-coming district of Bierzo it's the silky and perfumed local Mencia that's causing a stir.

Spanish whites are also charging ahead, with cooler northern regions making fresh aromatic whites that are proving far more exciting than the somewhat dull Airén that still dominates its white vineyards. In Rueda the whites are made from the local varieties Verdejo (Verdelho) and Viura, plus Sauvignon Blanc, while Rías Baixas is home to some intriguing whites from the crisp and minerally Albariño grape.

Spain's marvellous mezcla of wines also includes the generally simple, fresh and affordable sparkling Cavas, while in the deep south, Jerez lends its name to the country's great fortified wine, sherry (see page 92).

KEY GRAPE VARIETIES: TEMPRANILLO, AIRÉN, GARNACHA, MONASTRELL, CABERNET SAUVIGNON, MERLOT, ALBARIÑO, VERDEJO, MENCIA, GRACIANO, GODELLO, VIURA

GERMANY:
critical Riesling

Its reputation may have become somewhat sullied by some of the dilute sugary shockers of the past, but look beyond these and you'll see that Germany offers the greatest proliferation of pure and shining Riesling than any other nation.

As one of the coolest winegrowing countries, its wines tend to be white, light and crisp. Almost half of its vineyards are devoted to the white varieties, Riesling and Müller-Thurgau, with Riesling being the most important in terms of quality.

Many of these have alcohol levels as low as 7% and are made in a sweet style that can still taste wonderfully fresh due to the racy acidity provided by this cool climate. Dry examples can be identified by looking for the word Trocken on the label, with Halb Trocken sometimes used to indicate an off-dry style.

German wine labels can be difficult to decipher due to that country's complex system of classifying wines. When it comes to its quality wines (QmP), it's all based on levels of ripeness — with Kabinett the lightest style, Spätlese made from riper grapes, Auslese from even riper and later-picked grapes. Then you enter the realms of the ultra-sweet, with Beerenauslese made from individually selected berries affected by noble rot and the ultra-intense Trockenbeerenauslese.

Riesling reigns supreme in the northern regions of Rheingau, where it accounts for over 80% of the region's vineyards, and also in the Mosel, from which some of the world's most esteemed examples hail.

The climate in the south is a little warmer, which allows for the cultivation of more red grapes with the most important variety being Spätburgunder (Pinot Noir). In regions such as Baden-Württemberg, it makes a particularly light fresh version, but it is rarely seen outside the country.

KEY GRAPE VARIETIES: RIESLING, MÜLLER-THURGAU, SPÄTBURGUNDER (PINOT NOIR), SILVANER, DORNFELDER GRAUBURGUNDER (PINOT GRIS)

NEW WORLD ORDER

CHILE:

ripe pickings

Chile's most famous poet, Pablo Neruda, described his country as 'this strange sliver of geography', an apt analogy given this corridor of a country sandwiched between the sea and the mountains is around 4500km long and averages just 175km wide. However, it's only in a band of temperate land in the middle of the country where vines can be grown.

Chile's winemaking history dates back to the 16th century, when the Spanish conquistadors brought vines with them when they arrived to colonise the country. A considerable French influence followed in the 19th century, which precipitated the spread of Gallic grapes, such as Cabernet Sauvignon and Merlot, that still dominate Chilean vineyards today.

However, it wasn't until the 1980s that the country's modern wine industry got under way when new stainless steel tanks, which preserved the bright fruit that now characterises its wines, replaced the traditional rauli barrels that had left their mark of bitterness and astringency on the wines of the past.

Chile's wines now span the fresh aromatics grown in cooler

coastal and southern regions to the rich robust reds from the warmer central regions, with Chilean Sauvignon Blanc from Casablanca regarded as one of the world's main contenders for New Zealand's Sauvignon crown.

Carmenère has swiftly risen from obscurity to become Chile's flagship grape. After almost dying out in the vineyards of Bordeaux from where it originates, this variety with its darkly coloured, smooth and spicy wines with a signature savoury herbal note was found in abundance in Chile where it had been mistaken for Merlot.

With its warm climate, good growing conditions and cheap labour, Chile can produce great-value wines in ripe fruity styles, such as rich plush Merlot and Cabernet Sauvignon, expressive Shiraz, tropically fruited Chardonnay and expressive aromatics such as Viognier and Gewürztraminer.

KEY GRAPE VARIETIES: CARMENÈRE, MERLOT, CABERNET SAUVIGNON, CHARDONNAY, SAUVIGNON BLANC

ARGENTINA:
wines with altitude

Descriptions of Argentinean wines tend to be strewn with superlatives. Vines grow at over 3000 feet, making for some of the world's highest vineyards; its main wine province of Mendoza is possibly the world's largest fine-wine region, with vineyards covering almost six times the area of all of New Zealand's wine regions put together; while its population used to have one of the highest levels of per capita wine consumption.

It was only when locals started drinking less that Argentina — which ranks fifth in terms of global wine production — was forced to start exporting and transform its wines from rustic affairs into quality products designed to please international palates. Argentinean wine now ranges from extremely well-priced everyday examples characterised by an abundance of rich ripe fruit to an expanding number of promising top labels.

One of the secrets behind Argentina's key styles is in the different altitudes at which many of its vineyards are planted. At increased height the sunlight that aids ripening and concentration becomes more intense, while cool nights help retain freshness and aromatics and keep alcohol levels lower than might be expected from such a warm climate.

The country's flagship grape is Malbec. In France, it plays a minor part in Bordeaux blends and produces something quite different from its heartland in Cahors, but in Argentina it's found a highly suitable home where it makes rich, dark-fruited varietal wines that often exhibit an attractive violet-like perfumed element.

A wide range of European settlers have introduced a diverse offering of grape varieties, such as Cabernet Sauvignon, Syrah and Bonarda used in its reds and Pinot Gris and Torrontés in its whites — the latter a crisp and floral variety originally hailing from Spain, which like Malbec has found more favour here than in its heartland.

KEY GRAPE VARIETIES: MALBEC, TORRONTÉS, BONARDA, CABERNET SAUVIGNON, CHARDONNAY

SOUTH AFRICA:
big game

While technically a New World nation, with 350 years of winemaking behind it, South Africa has a distinctly, Old World feel. This extends to the style of its wines, which embody big ripe New World fruit, while often exhibiting an earthiness and elegance that allies them with the Old World.

It also has an abundance of different terrains: from hot inland areas to cool coastal and higher altitude sites. Considerable work has already been done to match grapes to the country's regions, which are producing a plethora of styles.

South Africa's wines have had a somewhat chequered history both at home and in New Zealand. After gaining a foothold in the market, by the time of the apartheid-related sanctions of the 1970s they had disappeared from New Zealand's shelves, only to return looking rather old-fashioned following the progress made by New World competitors such as Australia.

However, over the last decade, South Africa has upped its game, backed by considerable investment from foreign winemaking groups, and now produces modern wines with an Old World flavour.

Chenin Blanc has historically been the country's mainstay. In the past South African versions of this Loire variety could be somewhat neutral, but the best are edging ever closer to the intense tangy, minerally benchmark examples from the Loire.

Although far less widely planted than Chenin Blanc in South Africa, Pinotage is now the country's flagship grape. It produces a wide range of reds, from simple and lighter raspberry-fruited examples to those with a darker fruit profile and power when made from older vines in a premium region, such as Stellenbosch.

Bordeaux blends, the best of which can embody Old World elegance with the ripeness of New World fruit, are South Africa's other strong red suit, while its Shiraz is also starting to gain momentum and interest.

Given our loyalty to homegrown Sauvignon Blanc, we don't see many from South Africa on our shelves. However, increasingly impressive examples are now available as a result of the migration of plantings from the ill-suited warmer regions in which it was originally grown to cooler coastal regions and higher altitude sites.

KEY GRAPE VARIETIES: CHENIN BLANC, CABERNET SAUVIGNON, SHIRAZ, CHARDONNAY, SAUVIGNON BLANC, MERLOT, PINOTAGE

1 PINOT GRIS FROM FRANCE

SUGGESTED WINES

Greiner Alsace Pinot Gris, $25–27

Brecht Alsace Pinot Gris, $28–32

Domaine Albert Mann Alsace Pinot Gris, $32–36

TASTING NOTE: Alsace is the place to find the world's benchmark Pinot Gris. In this wine you should be able to smell and taste the variety's classic pear fruit and sweet spice, with more freshness than is often found from examples made elsewhere, and some real intensity of flavour. Sweetness can vary and you may pick up just a hint.

2

TEMPRANILLO/TEMPRANILLO BLEND FROM SPAIN

SUGGESTED WINES

Volver Paso a Paso, La Mancha, $15–20
Callejo Cuatro Meses en Barrique Ribera del Duero, $20–25
Cune Rioja Crianza, $25–30

TASTING NOTE: Running the spectrum from red to darker berries in different examples, these fruits are frequently joined in Tempranillo by savoury, earthy and leathery nuances. New American oak is often used on Rioja's Tempranillos in particular, imparting vanilla or sometimes coconutty flavours to its wines, which tend to be medium-bodied and velvety textured.

3 SANGIOVESE FROM ITALY

SUGGESTED WINES

Farnese Farneto Valley Sangiovese, $15–20

Majo di Norante Sangiovese, Abruzzo, $20–25

Villa Cafaggio Chianti Classico, $25–30

TASTING NOTE: Sangiovese's cherry berry fruit should be easy to identify in this wine, alongside savoury herbal notes and a fresh acidity. While lower-priced examples can be quite light, higher-end Sangiovese can be rich and succulent with considerable concentration.

4

CHILEAN CARMENÈRE

SUGGESTED WINES

Cono Sur Carmenère, $15–18

Concha Y Toro Casillero del Diablo Carmenère, $18–20

Viu Manent Secreto Carmenère, $20–25

TASTING NOTE: The supple fleshy blackberry and cherry fruit in this wine with its hints of dark chocolate indicate how easily it could be confused with Merlot. However, look out for the variety's herbal/green peppercorn characters.

5 ARGENTINEAN MALBEC

SUGGESTED WINES

Trapiche Estate Mendoza Malbec, $10–15

Bodega Septima Mendoza Malbec, $15–20

Chakana Reserve Malbec Lujan de Cuyo, Mendoza, $20–25

TASTING NOTE: The nose of Argentinean Malbec is often reminiscent of the smell of ink accompanied on the palate by plenty of big ripe brooding dark fruit. The colour and flavours are intense, but are backed by an attractive freshness.

6 SOUTH AFRICAN PINOTAGE/PINOTAGE BLEND

SUGGESTED WINES

Cape Bay Pinotage, $10–15

Goat's Do Roam Red, $15–20

Kaapzicht Pinotage, Stellenbosch, $20–26

TASTING NOTE: Blackberries and blueberries burst out of the nose, sometimes accompanied by a slight whiff of burnt rubber. Pinotage's body is on the fuller side, with alcohol levels often quite high, but in the best examples this is supported by wonderfully ripe fruit and savoury earthy notes enhanced by a light-handed use of spicy oak.

CHAPTER NINE

Perfect Pairings

'Great wine and food pairings, like great dinner parties, come from an assemblage of contrasting experiences and opinions.'

Cameron J Douglas, Master Sommelier, Auckland

From Fred and Ginger to Dolce & Gabbana; from wild duck and Pinot Noir to Sauvignon Blanc and goat's cheese, some pairings just spark a synergy that elevates the individual players to completely new levels. And when it comes to the marriage of food and wine, a good match can certainly propel your appreciation of both to new heights.

Despite all the tomes dedicated to the subject, it's not rocket science. It's more about common sense and thinking about the flavours, textures and weight of the food you're going to be eating and what might complement them.

Although most food and wine rub shoulders without too much disharmony, there are some combos that just don't go. Take asparagus for example; it can turn a full fruity red into something unpleasantly vegetal. And a bone-dry white will taste searingly sour when paired with a sweet dessert.

There are no hard-and-fast rules, although if you bear in mind the handful of key factors explored in this chapter and look at how some of the classic combinations work, you will be able to avoid truly hellish clashes and start coming up with your own heavenly marriages.

Never feel obliged to choose wine that you don't like just because it's touted as the best match with the dish you're eating. It's all about heightening enjoyment. So relax, have fun discovering what works — and what doesn't — and follow your own road through the fascinating practice of food and wine matching.

Matchmaking basics

WEIGHT AND BODY WATCHING

Something to take into account when making your matches is the perceived weight of the dish and the importance of pairing like with like. Rich wines can drown light foods, while conversely light wines can be overwhelmed by heavy dishes.

As well as the weight of a main ingredient such as chicken, also take into account the way in which it's cooked. For example, chicken when plainly grilled is considerably less weighty than when it's part of a richer stew like coq au vin, with the former demanding a white and the latter begging a heartier red.

INTENSITY AND FLAVOURS

Intensity is another important factor that's not to be confused with weight. Thai cuisine is a good example of one that's highly flavoured while actually being very light, often requiring a wine that's light in body, but with bags of flavour.

And don't forget the sauce; if it's the dominant part of the dish you should pay more attention to it than what lies beneath. An example might be a delicate fish served with hollandaise sauce — in which case you need to serve something with more oomph such as an oaked Chardonnay. A fresh lighter red might even be appropriate if the fish has been cooked in a really rich sauce.

When it comes to the specific flavours in a dish, these can often be enhanced by selecting a wine of the appropriate weight and intensity that exhibits similar flavours. The combination of asparagus and Sauvignon Blanc is a great example of such a match; the former's overt green notes create havoc with many wines, but harmonise with Sauvignon Blanc's vibrant, herby and sometimes asparagusy notes.

GETTING FRESH

Then there's the acidity of your dish to take into consideration. Sharp salad dressings, tomatoes, a squeeze of lemon or vinegared sushi rice can make many wines taste dull and flat. Dishes of this nature beg for varieties that have the acidity to meet them head on. It's also worth noting that crisp wines in general are able to lift the flavours of even a simple dish, making them the most 'food friendly' styles.

Acidity tends be higher in wines from cooler climates and in white varieties such as Riesling, Sauvignon Blanc, Chenin Blanc and cool-climate Chardonnay. Among the reds, Pinot Noir and Cabernet Sauvignon have relatively high levels of acidity, as do many varieties hailing from Italy, such as Sangiovese and Nebbiolo.

SWEET THINGS

Now on to sweeter things. When both sweet and sour are combined it creates a conundrum for most wines. However, sweeter styles of Riesling have the acid and sugar to survive the sensory onslaughts provided by this kind of sweet-savoury fare, while fruity off-dry rosés can come into their own.

When you are choosing a wine to complement dessert you need to find one with a comparable sugar content. It needs to be as sweet, if not sweeter, than the dish itself, or it will taste sour and thin.

GETTING A GRIP

Chewy textured tannin can be a tricky customer when it comes to teaming it with food. It reacts with the iodine found in many fish, making both wine and fish taste metallic. It also does egg dishes few favours, and undesirably emphasises the heat in hot dishes. However, tannic wines are best when they're rubbing up alongside red meat, where tannins bind to a meat's protein, particularly in something like rare steak, making them feel less forceful.

OPPOSITES ATTRACT

Some of the best matches are made when wine and food spark off each other through contrasts. For example, rich and fatty foods often work well with lighter bodied crisp wines, which cut through the fat. Bear in mind these will need to have enough intensity to stand up to the rich flavours of the food, which makes a variety such as Riesling highly suitable.

Salt and sweet are quite different tastes, but when juxtaposed in classic matches, such as a salty blue cheese with sweet wine,

WEIGHT CHART

Here's a rough guide to the weight of various grapes and styles, going from lightest to heaviest. However, weights do vary from place to place, with cooler regions producing lighter versions and warmer ones wines that are fuller bodied.

Whites: Riesling / Champagne-sparkling wines / Chenin Blanc / unoaked Chardonnay / Sauvignon Blanc / Pinot Gris / Gewürztraminer / Viognier / barrel-fermented Chardonnay

Reds: rosé / Beaujolais-Gamay / Pinot Noir / Rioja-Tempranillo / Grenache / Chianti-Sangiovese / Merlot / Syrah-Rhône blends / Cabernet-Malbec-Bordeaux blends / New World Shiraz

the combination can be sublime. Equally, while dry wine is a disaster with sweet foods, swap things around as in the match of foie gras and super-sweet Sauternes and you've got a winner.

But beware, opposites don't always attract. Star-crossed combos that are best avoided include sweet foods and dry wines as mentioned earlier, rich dishes with lightly flavoured wines, high acid dishes with low acid wines and hot or salty foods with tannic wines.

CLASSIC PARTNERSHIPS

Wine and food matching is something of a subjective business. Just as some people love peanut butter and jam sandwiches and others loathe them, certain matches will work better for individual palates, hence a number of wines being suggested here for each food.

Given the variation inherent in both the way dishes will be cooked and individual wines within the styles recommended, no match can ever be set in stone. However, this guide should provide an idea of the kind of wines that complement a variety of popular foods.

APPETISING ACCOMPANIMENTS

It's best to start on a light note with nibbles; fresh unoaked styles such as Riesling, Sauvignon Blanc or a sparkling wine are all great at getting the juices flowing before your meal. As appetisers have a tendency to be salty, skip the tannic reds at this stage, which can also tire the palate. A Fino or Manzanilla sherry will serve you far better.

PEARLS WITH SHELLFISH

The light texture and subtle flavours of shellfish suggest lighter wines to accompany them.

OYSTERS: their salty tang alongside a squeeze of lemon juice requires a light and fresh white, such as a cool-climate unoaked Chardonnay, a more restrained style of Sauvignon or a glass of fizz.

SQUID: let it get its tentacles around a fresh light white such as a dry Riesling or an unoaked Chardonnay.

MUSSELS: Marlborough's green-lipped mussels, when cooked with a strongly flavoured herb like coriander, will be a great match with the local Sauvignon Blanc; but choose a less intensely aromatic crisp dry white, such as an unoaked Chardonnay, when cooking them with more subtle flavourings.

SCALLOPS: these deserve a wine with a touch of sweetness or sweeter fruit, such as an off-dry Riesling or Pinot Gris or Viognier.

CRAB: serve this treat with a wine offering a bit more richness, such as Viognier, a riper Riesling or a top-notch Chardonnay.

LOBSTER: go for a bold white such as an oaked Chardonnay or Viognier, especially if the crustacean is slathered in a rich sauce.

PAUA: the intense flavours favour something robust, such as an oaked Chardonnay.

ALL THINGS FISHY

An axiom that's been unceremoniously overturned in recent years is the one dictating that you should only drink white wine with fish. To be fair, there's good reason behind this as the stronger character of many red wines can overpower the subtle flavours of some fish, and then there's the issue of the combination of certain fish and red wine turning each other metallic-tasting. However, meatier fish or those cooked in full-flavoured sauces often do go swimmingly with red wines.

LIGHTER WHITE FISH: the likes of john dory, orange roughy, gurnard, monkfish and tarakihi require more delicate white companions, with fresh unoaked whites such as Riesling, dry Pinot Gris and unoaked Chardonnay making great matches.

FULLER FLAVOURED WHITE FISH: snapper, mullet, groper and similar species need wines of a fuller bodied and flavoured framework, such as a sturdy Chardonnay, Sémillon or Arneis.

MEATY FISH: those with darker flesh and more intense flavours are able to handle red wines as well as more robust whites, e.g. salmon works well with a full dry white like Chardonnay, as well as a flavourful dry rosé and a lighter red such as Pinot Noir. And really meaty fish such as tuna pairs well with rosé or a soft red like Pinot Noir or Merlot.

POULTRY MATCHING

CHICKEN: the versatile chook can get chummy with bigger dry whites as well as lighter reds. Think oaked Chardonnay and a rich Pinot Gris, while Pinot Noir's the star among the reds, but even a mellow Merlot or Bordeaux blend can work wonderfully, especially when the bird has been cooked with herbs and other robust flavours.

DUCK: indisputably divine with Pinot Noir, this dish also flies high with Syrah/Shiraz and red Rhône blends, Merlot and even a sweeter Riesling, which will cut through the fat.

QUAIL: the dark flesh of this little bird is best accompanied by a mid-weight red, such as a Pinot, Merlot, or a Tempranillo or Sangiovese-based blend.

TURKEY: a big bird with powerful flavours that begs a similarly buxom wine, such as a fuller bodied Chardonnay with the breast and a mid-weight red like Pinot Noir, Merlot or Shiraz/Syrah with the darker leg meat.

PORKY PICKS

The comparatively lighter flavour of pork can make either a red or white an appropriate match. Whites need to be fuller, such as a warm-climate Chardonnay, although pork belly pairs marvellously with an off-dry Riesling, the freshness of which acts as a foil to its fat and works particularly well when apple or a combination of aromatic spices is present.

When served as a roast or as chops, a medium red is champion; think Pinot Noir, Grenache, Sangiovese or Tempranillo. And when it comes to bangers, a mid-weight red with an acid bite to balance any fat present in the sausages should be on the menu, such as a Chianti, a Rhône blend or a Syrah/Shiraz.

FAIR GAME

Gamey tastes can be enhanced when deliberately echoed in the accompanying wine; an earthy Pinot Noir, a leathery Syrah, a mature Bordeaux blend or a Barolo makes a winning combination, especially with wild boar.

RABBIT: runs riot with Pinot Noir, Rioja or a lighter style of Syrah/Shiraz.

VENISON: as the least gamey flavoured meat, it needs something with plenty of guts, such as a Syrah/Shiraz or Cabernet.

NOT BAAAD WITH LAMB

When roast or grilled lamb is on the menu, a mature Bordeaux blend is a brilliant match, as is an older Rioja. A soft Aussie Shiraz works well with stews, while a shepherd's pie sings alongside a Shiraz/Syrah Grenache blend.

BEEFED UP

Big flavours and textures call for big wines, and beef can take on the best. When serving steak, a medium- to full-bodied red works best, so bring out your finest Cabernet and Bordeaux blend, or a Syrah/Shiraz or Malbec to do the meat justice.

Ripe bold reds are the order of the day with stews: think Cabernet, Aussie Shiraz and Merlot. A beef roast should be paired with a similar-weighted wine, such as a Bordeaux blend.

And as for the humble beef burger, select an everyday red such as an Aussie Shiraz or local Merlot.

GOOD EGGS

While not the easiest combo to crack, an unoaked or lightly oaked Chardonnay is often the safest choice with egg-based dishes such as omelettes or fritters. A dry Pinot Gris or Pinot Blanc is also a good choice. Sparkling wines suit scrambled eggs, and if there's meat in the mix, then a lighter red such as a Pinot Noir or softer Merlot may be a tasty bet.

VEGETARIAN CUISINE

As a rule lighter, crisper whites are a vegetarian and vegetable-based cuisine's best friend. Fresh softer reds are good too, due to the lack of raw tannin-taming protein. However, when roasted, vegetables can stand up to fuller bodied fare, and when served with sauce consider the weight of the latter, which if dominant will need to be paid greater heed than the vegetables themselves.

A hearty red, particularly something Spanish, will usually love your lentils while a nutty white such as an oaked Chardonnay or Sémillon or even a peppery Aussie Grenache blend makes an excellent accompaniment to a nut roast.

ARTICHOKES: approach this vegetable with caution as it can make wines taste metallic or sweet. A dry tangy white such as a Sauvignon Blanc, unoaked Chardonnay or Grüner Veltliner should survive unscathed.

ASPARAGUS: absolutely classic with Sauvignon Blanc, but very little else.

AVOCADO: Sauvignon Blanc again comes up trumps with its acid zing to counter the fat content.

CAPSICUM: pair green ones with a crisp dry white, especially Sauvignon Blanc with its own vegetal notes, while red capsicums will be happier with wines containing a hint of sweetness, such as an off-dry Riesling or Pinot Gris.

KUMARA/PUMPKIN/SQUASH: these rich flavours can handle rich wines, such as a full oaky Chardonnay or an oily off-dry Pinot Gris.

MUSHROOMS: an older Pinot Noir, Rioja or Bordeaux blend if available will match the earthy tones. If cooked with garlic, though, go for a simpler soft red like a light Italian or everyday Shiraz.

SPINACH: this vegetable can bring out bitter or metallic notes in red wines in particular, although a lighter red like Pinot Noir is often able to cope.

SWEETCORN: nothing else needed but a big buttery Chardonnay.

TOMATOES: high acidity in tomatoes calls for a high acid wine, such as Sauvignon Blanc, cooler climate Chardonnay, simple young Pinots or fresh Italian reds.

RATATOUILLE: reach for a full-bodied wine like Shiraz, a crisp full-flavoured rosé or even a Sauvignon Blanc to match the dish's tomatoes and herbs.

SALADS: as most of these tend to be light with acid-based dressings, choose something with similar traits, such as a Sauvignon Blanc or Riesling, dry rosé (or light red for salads featuring meat). If served with a mayonnaise dressing, something weightier, such as an oakier Chardonnay or Viognier, is called for.

BARBIE BEAUTS

With food cooked over coals you need to haul in a wine with more intensity to match the charry edge. Big and bold blockbusting Aussie Shiraz and Shiraz Cabernet blends are perfect with barbecued meat, especially those with smoky and chilli-based marinades. The sweetness of sparkling Shiraz works amazingly well with sweeter barbecue sauces and as a light-hearted wine it's well suited to a barbecue's casual mood.

Those looking for a more refreshing option to provide contrast will enjoy an off-dry Riesling, Pinot Gris or that great all-rounder rosé which works especially well with citrus and herby marinades. Viognier or a big ripe Chardonnay with plenty of fruity sweetness are two whites that also bond well with barbecued foods.

GETTING SAUCY

When a sauce is an integral part of a dish, it becomes a supremely important factor when selecting a suitable wine.

EGG SAUCES: A white like Chardonnay rules the roost when it comes to partnering hollandaise and mayonnaise, or a Sauvignon if there's a twist of citrus.

TOMATO: a wine with good acidity is the thing, such as a Sauvignon Blanc; but if meat is involved, a fresh fruity Merlot will work well.

SALSA: a very hot salsa will numb your palate to the flavours of most wines, although a Sauvignon Blanc's worth a try, or a robust dry rosé.

CREAMY SAUCES: Chardonnay makes a classic accompaniment to this type of rich sauce.

VINEGAR-BASED SAUCES: serve with a high acid wine, such as an unoaked cool-climate Chardonnay, a Sauvignon or try a fresh Italian red.

THE SPICE IS RIGHT?

Highly spiced foods can result in some rather unappetising wine clashes, especially with tannic reds as spiciness accentuates bitter notes in this style of wine, while high-alcohol reds intensify the heat.

With more lightly spiced and aromatic cuisines, a spicy Gewürztraminer can be an asset, pairing particularly well with ginger, as will a Pinot Gris with a touch of sweetness or fellow aromatics Riesling and Sauvignon Blanc.

Chilli numbs the taste buds, so never waste fine wine on a meal containing liberal amounts. A simple chilled white can act as a refreshing foil, but most wines will be overwhelmed by really hot stuff.

Thai spices tend to work with a tangy wine like Sauvignon Blanc, which can echo notes of lemongrass and coriander. Cool-climate Chardonnay and dry sparkling wine are other excellent options, while red wines are probably best avoided.

Fresh and fruity wines, such as sparkling, rosé, Gewürztraminer and Pinot Gris are all able partners to cooler curries. For the fieriest, a chilled soft fruity light red is the best, but sometimes it's better to avoid wine altogether and go for a beer or traditional Indian yoghurt-based lassi.

NOT SO EASY CHEESY

Cheese and wine have long been considered the classic combination but cheese can be wine's nemesis. Research has found that cheese can actually dull a wine drinker's palate, most probably due to proteins in the cheese binding to a wine's flavour

KIWI COMBINATIONS

FISH AND CHIPS: a crisp white such as a Riesling, an unoaked Chardonnay or even something sparkling.

MEAT PIE: choose a Merlot or Shiraz as you need a soft red with some nice density of fruit.

WHITEBAIT FRITTER: the egg content demands a more buttery wine, such as a lightly oaked Chardonnay or Pinot Gris.

SAUSAGE ROLL: an easy drinking Italian red such as Montepulciano d'Abruzzo, a light Merlot or even a Shiraz — the choice is yours with the humble sausage roll.

PAVLOVA: a sweet sparkling wine, particularly Asti, makes a superb accompaniment to our national dessert.

molecules or as a result of the gluey textured fat from the cheese coating the mouth, deadening the taster's perception of a wine's flavours.

Although this seemingly idyllic marriage may have been exposed as something of a sham, there are still some pleasing potential partnerships.

HARD: cheddar and tasty cheese both pair well with medium- to full-bodied reds including Bordeaux blends, Merlot, Chianti and even a full Aussie or Gisborne Chardonnay, while Parmesan or other mature cheeses respond to a soft, fresh and fruity wine, such as a Chianti or a lighter Merlot.

SOFT: milder soft cheeses call for milder wines, such as an unoaked Chardonnay with creamy notes. Camembert is notoriously difficult to match, but a mellow Merlot or soft Pinot Noir — nothing with too much tannin — can work well. There are some truly inspirational unions to be had, such as the pairing of Alsace's classic über stinky Munster cheese and Gewürztraminer.

GOAT'S CHEESE: loves a crisp dry white, with Sauvignon Blanc an undisputed classic combination.

BLUE CHEESE: Port and Stilton is a celebrated match, but this kind of dense salty blue cheese can also shine with mellow reds like Coonawarra Cabernet and New Zealand Merlot, while hard creamier Roquefort styles are sublime with a rich sweet botrytis-affected sticky.

THE PUDDING CLUB

Desserts can be among the most difficult dishes to partner wine with. Some people opt out at this point, preferring to drink a glass of dessert wine on its own rather than embarking upon the seemingly near-impossible task of trying to find a wine of at least equal sweetness required for true harmony.

The trick is to pick a wine that's sweeter than the dish you plan to serve, which can be a hard ask as most dessert wines are markedly lower in sugar content than the majority of puddings. However, here are some palatable pairings.

FRUIT-BASED DESSERTS: good with a medium-sweet Riesling or Chenin.

CREAMY EGGY CONFECTIONS: match desserts such as crème brûlée, custard-based dishes and cheesecake with a sweet noble Sémillon.

LEMON TART: a noble Chenin or Riesling can comfortably match the sweetness and citrus kick of this classic tart.

CHOCOLATE: with its gooey texture and high sugar content, chocolate has been the death of many a wine. Go for a sweet sparkling style if it's a fairly lightweight dessert or a botrytised Sémillon if it's heavier. Its richest elaborations require something full-on, with fortifieds such as Australia's liqueur Muscats, some of the few to have the affinity and power to partner the richest chocolate desserts.

RICH FRUITCAKE/CHRISTMAS PUDDING: serve with a light sweet sparkling Muscat for an interesting contrast, or match like with like with a rich sweet fortified wine such as a Rutherglen Muscat, a Madeira or sweet sherry.

ICE CREAM AND SORBETS: the palate-numbing properties of frozen desserts do nothing for wine and are best served solo.

If you still want to drink a Cabernet with your crayfish or a Sauvignon with your steak, then by all means go ahead. However, swap these pairings around and your enjoyment of both should be greatly enhanced.

For this tasting prepare some bite-sized portions of the foods suggested and see how well they pair with the recommended wines and match or clash with the other wines in this tasting. You can also add a cheese platter to create more combinations.

1

SUPERB WITH SEAFOOD

Select something light, fresh and citrusy like an Albariño from Spain or a zesty local Riesling.

SUGGESTED WINES

Martin Codax Rías Baixas Albariño, Spain, $20–25

Viña Almirante Pionero Mundi Rías Baixas Albariño, Spain, $20–25

Lagar de Cervera Rías Baixas Albariño, Spain, $35–45

TASTING NOTE: See how this light-bodied wine with its fresh lemony and minerally notes complements rather than overpowers the subtle flavours of fish. It also has the acidity that makes it able to handle a twist of lemon.

2

NICE WITH SPICE — PINOT GRIS

SUGGESTED WINES

Woollaston Tussock Nelson Pinot Gris, $15–20
Terrace Heights Estate Marlborough Pinot Gris, $20–25
Bilancia Hawkes Bay Pinot Gris, $25–30

TASTING NOTE: The spice in this variety echoes the aromatics in many spicy dishes and stands up to them — just as long as they're not too hot.

3

SUITED TO ASPARAGUS — SAUVIGNON BLANC

SUGGESTED WINES

Eradus Marlborough Sauvignon Blanc, $15–20

Jules Taylor Marlborough Sauvignon Blanc, $20–25

Dog Point Sauvignon Blanc, $25–30

TASTING NOTE: A great example of a wine mirroring the strong flavours in a food. Sauvignon's green notes go well with asparagus, but try the vegetable with a red wine and sample a combination that's positively detrimental!

4

DIVINE WITH DUCK — PINOT NOIR

SUGGESTED WINES

Elbows Bend Central Otago Pinot Noir, $15–20
Carrick Unravelled Central Otago Pinot Noir, $20–30
Mount Dotterel Central Otago Pinot Noir, $30–40

TASTING NOTE: This wine's bright acidity cuts through the duck's fat, while its gamey savoury notes echo the flavours of its meat. Add a cherry sauce comparable to the wine's flavours and you've got one marvellous match!

5

A MATCH FOR MEAT

Reds with some structure are suited to darker meats such as steak: think Cabernet, Syrah/Shiraz and Malbec.

SUGGESTED WINES

A Rhône-style blend such as La Vieille Ferme Côtes du
   Ventoux, France, $15–20
Château Nicot Bordeaux, France, $20–25
Newton Forrest Hawke's Bay Malbec, $25–35

TASTING NOTE: Try the wine by itself before having it with the meat and see the way the meat mitigates the astringent effect of its tannins. Bold flavours and big textures meet each other here head on.

6

A SWEET FOR YOUR SWEET

Choose a light- to medium-sweet dessert wine, such as a late harvest wine or sweeter style of Riesling.

SUGGESTED WINES

Alpha Domus Pilot Leonarda Late Harvest Hawke's Bay
  Semillon, $15–20

Muddy Water Waipara Riesling Unplugged, $20–27

Pyramid Valley Growers Series Lebecca Vineyard Marlborough
  Riesling, $27–30

TASTING NOTE: Try this wine with desserts of differing sweetness levels. Rich chocolate puddings and the like will overwhelm this style of wine, which comes into its own with lighter fruit-based dishes.

CHAPTER TEN

Selecting, Storing and Serving

'Forget fashion: focus on wines which resonate with you and try to think of flavours and styles in terms of regions and terroir.'

Neil McCallum, Dry River, Martinborough

It's time to go shopping! But before setting out, let's look at the many options available to wine buyers today and see where to find wines of real interest and value, while avoiding the duds and the dull stuff.

Selecting

THE PRICE IS RIGHT?

We all have a sweet spot, where the price we're prepared to pay for our wine corresponds with the quality we're after. While some are prepared to fork out $5000 for a bottle of Château Pétrus, one of the world's most expensive wines, for others $15 is more their ballpark. Wine prices cover a huge range, but what exactly are you paying for?

In the case of Château Pétrus, it's a luxury brand just like Rolex or Rolls-Royce, with its price based on prestige, a couple of centuries of winemaking expertise and high demand for its limited supply.

The actual cost of producing the wine is a tiny percentage of the price tag of most expensive wines. This is also true at the other end of the price spectrum, where packaging can account for a greater proportion of a cheaper wine's price than the liquid within it, given the low cost of the grapes that make it. This means both the cheapest and most expensive wine are far from bargains.

A multitude of factors influence price. Grapes ripen better in warmer countries giving more grapes per vine, making the resulting wine cheaper, while wines from cooler climes compensate for this by being able to command higher prices through making higher quality examples. This is why warm-climate wines from the likes of Australia dominate our lower shelves, while our homegrown products populate higher price brackets.

How a wine is made has a significant impact on price. Processing large volumes in big tanks is relatively cheap, while making small batches in expensive oak barrels is a far pricier option. Then there are the costs of bottling, packaging, distribution and marketing as well as other overheads. And at the end of the day, a winery's profits can often be a single-figure percentage of the bottle's final price.

Then before GST, there is the retailer's mark-up, which adds around another 30–35%, with restaurants taking somewhere between 100–300%. These margins may sound high, but are actually at the lower end internationally in a labour-intensive industry where few are making big bucks.

BARGAIN BUYS

Most wines reflect these costs and quality rises with price. However, there are still bargains that can be bagged, while some seemingly great deals may not be as good as they appear.

DISCOUNTED WINE: as the wine market gets more competitive we see more highly discounted wine on the shelves. However, with discounting increasingly becoming the norm, some brands are now being created at false price points, with their true value being closer to the marked down price than its full shelf price. To avoid disappointment, stick to trusted names that you know will deliver the goods at their full price.

BRAND OR BLAND?

Many people stick with the big brands, considering them a reliable and consistent option. This is generally true and many are pleasant enough wines that have often benefited from economies of scale. However, given that a sizeable chunk of their price will be for marketing rather than the cost of the wine in the bottle, they don't necessarily offer the best value for money. Made on an industrial scale with the mass-market palate in mind, they certainly rarely offer the most interest.

BIN ENDS: these are wines an outlet wants to clear. If they're simply ends of lines, maybe at the change of vintage, then they can be bargains. However, if they've ended up on special because they've been hard to shift, or have been gathering dust on hot shelves for years as they pass out of their prime, they may not be such a steal.

INTERNET DEALS: wines sold online can cut out a chunk of distributor and retailer costs. Some of these operations act as a channel through which wineries can offload surplus stock, offering sharp deals on often highly quaffable wines.

SURPLUS STOCK: in countries where supply is greater than demand, prices are forced to drop, resulting in some particularly well-priced wines. This has happened in Australia during recent years, and is starting to occur here too as a result of a larger vintages.

CLEANSKINS: these unlabelled wines often offered at knock-down prices are the product of wineries that would prefer us not to know they've got too much stock to sell at full price. These can be good value or real shockers. Take a chance if you dare!

SEASONAL BUYING: many of the best deals are on offer over Christmas, so if you've got the cash spare it's a great time to stock up.

BULK ORDERS: buying by the case can often mean saving money. If you can't get through a case by yourself, club together with some friends and share the spoils.

UNDISCOVERED TERRITORY: wineries and regions that are still underneath the radar are often far more competitively priced than those that have already made their name. For example, instead of buying a Rioja, choose a wine from the lesser-known Campo de Borja and save dollars. And keep your ear to the ground about exciting new producers who've yet to make it big.

DECIPHERING THE LABEL

When it comes to working out what a label's telling you on a wine made in a country such as France or Germany, you might feel that you need to be a Master of Wine to make sense of it! However, most New Zealand wine labels are relatively straightforward, although it's worth paying close attention to ensure you're getting exactly what you want. The key elements to note are:

BRAND/PRODUCER: while you can rely on some names to produce good wines year in year out, it's also worth experimenting with names you don't know.

GRAPE VARIETY: in New World wines, this information often features prominently, providing an idea of the style of wine.

REGION/APPELLATION: in the case of wine from European nations, this information often takes the place of the grape variety, so you have to know something about the grapes grown in the regional appellation to deduce what's in the bottle. The region also gives an indication of a wine's style.

In many of the long-established winemaking countries, the regional designation is part of the nation's quality wine classification system, which you will see on the label, e.g. Denominazione di Origine Controllata (DOC) and the higher Denominazione di Origine Controllata e Garantita (DOCG) on Italian wines and Denomiaciónes de Origen (DO) and the loftier Denomiación di Origen Calificada (DOCa) on Spanish.

In France's elaborate Appellation Contrôllée (AOC) system, the more specific the regional designation, in theory the higher quality the wine. For example, in a region such as Burgundy the lowest-level appellation wines are simply labelled 'Bourgogne' (Burgundy), while the highest feature the name of a single vineyard, such as Le Montrachet, and assume you will be able to distinguish a region from a village from an individual site!

ALCOHOL LEVEL: this can be as low as 7% on German wines to over 15% on some bruisers from warm nations like Australia and South Africa — worth noting if you don't want to get squiffy after a glass or two. Wines with alcohol levels below 12% will often have some sweetness.

VINTAGE: the year in which the grapes for a wine were harvested (see page 122). Avoid older vintages on whites such as Sauvignon Blanc that don't tend to age well and with a few years on them may be past their prime.

Other information you might see on a label:

ADDITIVES: New Zealand law requires wineries to state that the wine contains sulphites (see page 106) as well any potential allergens from fining, with dairy or fish-based products.

STANDARD DRINKS: this is a guideline to assist drinkers in making judgements about their levels of alcohol consumption based on the measure of 10g of alcohol per standard drink.

RESERVE: while many Reservas from Spanish regions and the Riservas of Italy have minimum ageing requirements set down in law, in most other places the term has no teeth. While it suggests the wine is likely to have been a better batch set aside for later release with longer oak ageing, this is not always the case.

NOBLE: suggests the grapes this wine was made from were affected by noble rot (see page 89), resulting in a sweet and usually high-quality wine.

> Whether it costs you
> $15 or $150, a good
> wine is simply one that
> you enjoy.
>
> Ian Isaacs,
> Scenic Cellars, Taupo

SHOP TILL YOU DROP

When buying wine today, shoppers are spoilt for choice. From the convenience of the supermarket to the specialist service offered by the independent wine merchant, from the handily situated local liquor store to e-tailers offering smart deals online, there's an outlet for everyone and for every occasion.

NOT SO SUPERMARKETS

An estimated eight out of every 10 bottles of wine are now bought in the supermarket, making the latter by far New Zealand's most popular place to purchase wine. Supermarket wine sales have been driven by the convenience of popping a few bottles in the trolley during the big shop.

On the surface, the shelves of the supermarket wine aisles appear to be groaning with choice. Look a little closer and you'll find many of the labels are supplied by the big companies, increasingly the only ones able to offer the sharp prices and promotional funds demanded by the supermarkets for a listing.

In the absence of anyone available to advise customers on their wine selections, many purchases are made purely on price, with supermarkets generally able to offer products more cheaply, given the major buying muscle of the country's two major grocery groups.

LOCAL DRAW FOR THE LIQUOR STORE

The location of many liquor stores is often a stronger selling point than the range of wines on offer, which tends to be in the bargain booze end of the market making it rather limited.

The larger chains offer a wider selection of wines, although this is usually limited to mainly local and Australian lines and staff knowledge of the products depends on the individual branch. Those with more enlightened management offer more exciting selections beyond the mainstream staples most often seen in this kind of store, as well as ensuring their employees are more clued-up on the finer points of the wines they stock.

INDEPENDENTS' DAY

If you're after interesting wines and knowledgeable staff, then head to an independent wine shop. Often hand-picked for their quality and interest, the range of wines to be found in many of these smaller outlets can be wide, more eclectic and less likely to disappoint.

Driven by passion and not purely by profit, those involved with these smaller stores generally have an intimate knowledge of the wines they're selling. Well positioned to offer advice, they are often skilled at building long-term relationships with their customers whose tastes they get to know, making them adept at suggesting new wines they're likely to appreciate.

We're lucky to have a wealth of independent wine merchants in New Zealand (see page 241), many of whom regularly share their knowledge by running in-store tastings. A few specialise in one area, such as in French wines, others focus on less mainstream selections of local wines, while some list lines from both home and abroad.

WINE ONLINE

For those not wanting to leave their armchair, wine is just a mouse click away with the recent rise of the online retailer (see page 252). Some of these sites are the Internet arm of independent merchants, while others are stand-alone operations.

Many offer a wide selection of interesting wines accompanied by helpfully accurate descriptions.

> ‘Please don't be afraid to accept or ask for advice from the staff. Be prepared to try something new or outside your comfort zone and never be afraid to discuss price with the sommelier.'
>
> Chris Upton, O'Connell Street Bistro, Auckland

UP FOR AUCTION

Most wines for sale in the shop are from current vintages. However, for those seeking aged delights and the odd bargain or two, auction houses are worth checking out, with some offering bidding online.

DINING OUT

'Why don't they just give us a trigonometry quiz with the menu?' asked US comedian Jerry Seinfeld, exasperated at the complex wine lists which he felt only served to remind him that he had no idea what he was doing.

In New Zealand, it's rare to find the leather-bound tomes boasting hundreds of wines that can be found in countries with a long-established fine dining scene. However, selecting from any wine list can be daunting, with diners often opting for something they know thus missing out on the opportunity to try one of the gems on a good wine list.

Don't be afraid to ask for assistance: even the most experienced aficionados aren't afraid to do so as they know an experienced waiter will have an extensive knowledge of the menu and is consequently well placed to suggest good wine matches. While there are very few restaurants in New Zealand that have a dedicated sommelier — the French name for a wine waiter — any good establishment should have someone on hand who's able to guide you through the list to find a wine to suit your taste, your meal and your budget.

With their relatively modest corkage charges, restaurants offering BYO options are a great way to save money by avoiding mark-ups or provide the opportunity for you to savour your own special wines outside the home. While some restaurants are 100% BYO, others allot specific nights where this practice is allowed. Selecting a wine before you've set eyes on the menu can be a challenge, but if you can scope out the menu in advance — or at least have an idea of the cuisine — you can choose a style that should suit (see page 185).

RETURNING WINE

If the i-pod you've just purchased doesn't play, or the butter you've bought is rancid, chances are you'd feel confident in returning the product. But when people think the wine they've bought tastes a bit dodgy, many of them lack the confidence to take it back.

If you detect any of the nasties detailed in Chapter Five (see page 111), do return the bottle. While screwcapped wines have eliminated the most common culprit of cork taint, they can still have their issues. Poor storage can madeirise — heat damage — a wine, making it taste dull. Oxidation can also be an issue where the seal has been broken prior to the final twist or when buying wine by the glass — in bars in particular — when a wine has been left open way too long.

If you suspect something's up with the wine, rather than simply passing it off as one you don't like, get someone at its place of purchase to give it a try. More often than not they'll realise what's wrong and should be happy to exchange it for a bottle or glass in better condition.

Storing

In this age of instant gratification, most wines are polished off within 24 hours of purchase. Few of us take the time to cellar our wines, but those with the patience to squirrel away some well-chosen bottles can reap rich rewards in following a wine down a fascinating path from youthful exuberance to mellow old age.

That said, the majority of modern wines are made to be enjoyed young. Some from the classic wine regions of Europe have the 'bones' to last for a while, but most mainstream homegrown Sauvignon Blanc, Chardonnay, Pinot Gris and rosé in particular are often safest consumed a year or so after release.

Most reds benefit from a year or so in the bottle, while Riesling, Pinot Noir, Syrah and Bordeaux blends are more suited to laying down. However, it's not just the grape that makes a wine suitable for ageing, but also the quality. It needs to be balanced, with good intensity, acidity and in reds, a decent tannic structure, too. These qualities are generally only found in wines made from low-cropped vines, thus most commercial and cheaper wines just won't go the distance.

When you've made your selection, don't plonk your wines in the garage or in a rack in the kitchen. With their general fluctuations in temperature, these are the worst places to stash your cases or indeed keep any wine over even relatively short periods of time.

Constant temperature is the most important consideration

when finding a place to store your prized bottles, somewhere between 10–13°C is ideal. As UV is the enemy of wine — hence the coloured glass used for many bottles — seek out a dark place with minimal vibrations as agitation is not good for quality in long-term storage.

If you're going to be ageing wines over a long period of time, the presence of some humidity is important to stop corks drying out. This can also be assisted by keeping the bottles horizontal so that the liquid is in contact with the cork. However, in the medium term this isn't a major concern and is irrelevant when the wine's under screwcap.

If you've got good wines and nowhere suitable to store them, you could splash out on a temperature-controlled wine cabinet, although these are pretty pricey. There are also establishments that can look after your wines for you, particularly useful if you're buying them as an investment where a wine's provenance affects its price.

But if they've been bought to be drunk, don't forget to do just that! If you start to build up a large collection, it can get out of control and you may miss out on drinking them at their peak. In the case of larger collections, cellar software that can be used to catalogue, locate and even flag up wines that are ready for drinking is useful for keeping on top of your bottles.

Older wines can be wonderful, but wines are still definitely better cracked open when slightly too young than when they're way past their prime.

FINDING THE VALUE OF OLDER WINES

Most standard wines deteriorate rather than improve with lengthy ageing. If you've uncovered some long-forgotten old bottles open one and see for yourself. But if it's something more special, check it out before opening on the New Zealand-based online search engine www.wine-searcher.com, and see what similar wines are selling for. But you'll only get top dollar if they've been stored properly.

Serving

PUT ON YOUR GLASSES

In the same way great music sounds so much better through a surround-sound system than a tinny boom box, good wine can really be enhanced when drunk from a decent receptacle.

Shape is an important factor when selecting wine glasses, with a tapering bowl helping to concentrate aromas, something particularly pertinent to aromatic whites and the more perfumed reds. Clarity is another consideration. If you want to appreciate a wine's colour avoid opaque, frosted or tinted vessels in favour of plain crystal, which is more reflective as well as being clear. Its thin lip also delivers a better flow of wine across the palate.

Size is definitely important when it comes to stemware. Tiny glasses make the swirling required to release aromas out of a decent-sized pour nigh on impossible. For me, 350ml is the minimum volume for a wine glass — which should be poured to around a third full — and ideally a larger glass for reds that require more aeration.

For sparkling wines avoid the 'coupe', the saucer-shaped glass allegedly modelled on Marie Antoinette's breast. Rapidly dissipating a wine's sparkle, this glass arguably makes a better bra than bubbly glass, with the classic flute a far better choice.

There are now glasses designed to suit a wide range of grape varieties and styles, a tailor-made approach pioneered by Austrian glassmakers Riedel. There's even a breathable glass made by Eisch that claims to aerate a wine in a similar way to decanting.

However, for most, a set of reasonable quality standard glasses will suffice. A great multi-purpose glass is Zerutti's Ultimo Taster, while Riedel's Ouverture Magnum — now used at a number of New Zealand wine competitions — and Spiegelau's Authentis range are also good all-rounders. And if these are beyond your budget, designs that fit the basic shape criteria can also be found in most home stores.

WHEN TO DECANT

The decanter is not solely a receptacle for granny's fetid fortified wine, nor is the practice of decanting wine the prerogative of some pompous élite. There are many instances when wines of varied types will benefit from decanting.

Old reds often throw a deposit, which is not ideal if it makes the wine cloudy or gives the wine a granular texture. This can be dealt with through separating the wine from its sediment by decanting.

In the case of young reds, decanting can soften its rough edges and open it up. In all types of wine it can also help blow off moderate cabbage-like sulphide characters (see page 111).

When decanting a wine with sediment, ideally store the bottle upright for a week or so to allow it to fall to the bottom. Then pour the wine gently into a decanter stopping just before you reach the sediment. To aerate without any sediment, just vigorously tip it into the decanter.

There are plenty of fancy decanters available, the aesthetics of which can impart a sense of occasion to drinking a wine, but basically any old jug will do.

KEEPING OPENED BOTTLES

While there are a number of gizmos promoting themselves as wine-preservation aids, at home the fridge is still the best place in which to keep your opened vino. Lower temperatures slow chemical reactions and inhibit the production of vinegar-forming acetic bacteria, meaning a re-corked (or re-screwed) bottle in the fridge should last for up to three days. A far longer life can be guaranteed by the Enomatic machines, mechanised wine-serving systems that are slowly spreading through the country's wine establishments. These use a blanket of nitrogen to prevent opened wines from oxidising, keeping them fresh for up to three weeks.

TEMPERATURE CONTROL

'My dear girl, there are some things that are just not done, such as drinking Dom Perignon, '53 above the temperature of 38° Fahrenheit — that's as bad as listening to the Beatles without earmuffs.' 007 hit the mark — the temperature a wine is served at is important and too often incorrect.

From ice-cold whites to tepid reds, many wines are served at the wrong temperature. Most whites are best served from 6°C for lighter and sparkling styles, and up to 15°C for the finest and fullest examples. As the palate is numbed under 5°C and most domestic fridges run at below 6°C (beer fridges often even lower), the majority of wines served straight from the fridge are far too cold.

Muting aromas and masking flavours by over-chilling may be a remedy for making a bad bottle more bearable, but does little to enhance the enjoyment of a good wine.

Most whites do well with a mere hour in the fridge; if it's been in longer, pull it out around half an hour before it's going to be drunk to warm up slightly. When you need to chill wine fast, don't be afraid to throw it in the freezer for half an hour; but don't forget about it because wine that's been frozen is only fit to use in cooking.

We're often advised that red wines should be served at room temperature. However, the temperatures in your home on a sweltering summer's day, warmed by a heat pump or in a sweaty bar, are way too hot to make most reds taste that great. Heat releases the bouquet and softens red wines, but too much heat and it feels dull, flabby and alcoholic.

Optimum temperatures for reds are 15–19°C, with fuller and tannic reds at the top end. The bottle should feel slightly cool to

> I've no doubt that music affects your ability to perceive things differently, and that includes wine.
>
> Jeff Sinnott, Amisfield Winery

the touch. If it's warm, give it half an hour in the fridge or ask for an ice bucket if you're in a restaurant. Given the lingering preconceptions among many people that red wine should never be chilled, this advice may raise a few eyebrows but it will result in your wine tasting far better. Some lighter reds such as Beaujolais or a simple fruity Pinot Noir can also be enjoyed lightly chilled.

At the end of the day, it's best to serve a wine on the cold side rather than too hot as it's far easier to warm it up in the glass than cool it down. Ice cubes are not an option unless you want to dilute or disguise a particularly gruesome glassful.

ENTERTAINING WITH STYLE

When planning a dinner party, try and match your menu with some suitable wines (see page 186). A good rule of thumb is to move from light- to fuller bodied wines as the meal progresses.

For buffets or when a wide range of food will be on offer, it's best to opt for wines that will go with a wide variety of foods. Choose something fresh, fruity and versatile such as a drier Pinot Gris, a lightly oaked Chardonnay or a Pinot Noir.

Half a bottle per person is usually enough for most soirées and three-quarters often more than adequate — unless your guests drink like fish, then you might have to take control of the pouring or stash away some spare bottles to be used in a vinous emergency.

Keep your best wine for dinner parties and provide crowd-pleasing quaffing wine for bigger get-togethers where good wines can often get lost in the midst of larger-scale conviviality.

WINE AND MUSIC MATCHING

While the synergies between well-matched food and wine have long been recognised, studies now suggest the same may well be true of wine and music. Research conducted by the UK's Heriot Watt University discovered music has the power to considerably alter the way a wine's flavour was perceived. Those in the study rated a white wine 40% more zingy and refreshing when accompanied by a light piece of music, while a powerful and heavy piece made a red wine seem 60% stronger and richer than when sampled in silence. According to the American winemaker and technologist Clark Smith, who has conducted his own extensive research into this subject, we associate different wine types with different moods. When the feel of the wine and music are in accord, both improve. 'Red wines tend to be enhanced by soulful music, while cheerful or strident tones bring out harshness in reds, but complement fresh whites,' he says. It could be that the table settings of tomorrow will come not only with knife, fork, spoon and wine glass, but with an i-pod too!

CHEAP AND CHEERFUL

Go for under $15 wines from lesser-known producers and wine regions for a greater chance of your 'cheapie' being cheerful.

SUGGESTED WINES

Sarments de la Tuilerie, Costières de Nîmes, France, $10–15
Coto de Hayas Crianza, Campo de Borja, Spain, $10–15
Henry's Drive Pillar Box Red, Australia, $10–15

TASTING NOTE: At this price point you wouldn't expect to get earth-moving wines, but those offering the best value can offer eminently gluggable fresh and fruit-filled options.

2

BIG BRAND

See how a big brand stacks up against the first wine you tried from a smaller producer.

SUGGESTED WINES

Penfolds Rawsons Retreat Shiraz Cabernet, Australia, $10–15

Jacob's Creek Shiraz Cabernet, Australia, $10–15

Hardys Nottage Hill Shiraz, Australia, $10–15

TASTING NOTE: As you've probably picked up by now, big brands are slickly made with quite acceptable levels of fruit and freshness. However, they can lack character, although some are more interesting than others.

3

RESERVE

See what you get when you pay a few more dollars from the same big name.

SUGGESTED WINES

Penfolds Koonunga Hill Shiraz Cabernet, Australia, $15–20
Jacob's Creek Reserve Shiraz, Australia, $15–20
Hardys Oomoo Shiraz, Australia, $15–20

TASTING NOTE: It's a shame that some drinkers never take the next step up as they can often offer a considerable leap in quality and interest. Note the greater intensity found in this wine, about which you'll probably find more interesting characters to note.

4 COMPLEX AND CHARACTERFUL

Wines over $30 should start to offer something
pretty special. Here are suggestions for some
impressive and eclectic wines. Your local
independent wine shop should also be a good
source for some ideas for more intriguing bottles.

SUGGESTED WINES

Domaines des Baumard, Clos de Saint Yves Savennières, Loire,
France, $30–40

Descendientes De J Palacios Petalos del Bierzo, Beirzo, Spain,
$30–40

Dada 1, New Zealand, $40–50

TASTING NOTE: Linger over the special wine you've selected.
You should find plenty to say about its intriguing aromas and
captivating palate. Note the way its impression remains in
your mouth, and indeed your mind, long after swallowing.

5 AGED BEAUTY

Most wines in the shops are relatively recent vintages. However, some Spanish reds are released with more time in the bottle along with a handful of local wines kept back until they've got a bit of bottle age. Specialist retailers and auction houses are often a source of older wines. But if you've got something you've squirrelled away yourself this would also be a great time to bring it out.

SUGGESTED WINES

An older Spanish red such as Chivite Gran Feudo Reserva
  Navarra, Spain, $20–25
Matariki Hawke's Bay Quintology, $25–40
Puriri Hills Estate, Clevedon, $35–45

TASTING NOTE: Note how the fruit has fallen back in this wine to be replaced by notes more in the spectrum of spice, forest floor and mushroom. Tannins, which may have been quite grippy when young, will have softened, with the wine becoming a far mellower proposition. If a wine has got too old these secondary characters will not be enough to carry it and it will feel dried out with its alcohol too apparent.

CHAPTER ELEVEN

Put Your Taste to the Test

'Try as many different wines as you can. It doesn't matter if you strike wines that aren't your cup of tea, the joy is in the learning.'

Ryan Quinn, Wine Direct, Auckland

In 1976 the world of wine was rocked when some internationally unknown labels from California trounced some of France's most celebrated wines in a blind tasting. The Judgement of Paris, as this came to be known and which has since been the basis of two feature films, illustrates how when all the cues provided by packaging to a wine's provenance are removed, the playing field is levelled and some surprising results can ensue.

Everyone brings preconceptions to a wine, from knowing something about the producer or having tried their wines before, the look of the label, or the price. In fact one recent American study found that the more a wine costs, the more people enjoy it, regardless of how it tastes. This is due to the expectation that a higher-priced wine will be of a higher quality, which can actually trigger pleasure receptors in the brain!

In forcing you to leave all your assumptions at the door, tasting blind is one of the best ways to judge a wine impartially. While it might conjure up images of wine snobs parading their knowledge as they attempt to identify a wine right down to the location of the row of grapes from which it was made — something even ultra-experienced tasters can't often do — it's great fun and can be made into a convivial game if you want to inject an element of competition.

And now that you've read and tasted your way through the preceding chapters, you should be ready to put your knowledge to the test. A blind tasting is a great way to do this — and maybe see some of your own preconceptions overturned, too!

Holding a blind tasting

There's no blindfold required. A blind tasting works by obscuring the wine's identity, not removing your sight. The basic set-up is much the same as any other tasting, but with just a bit more organisation. Six wines is a good number as this will provide enough examples for comparisons and interest, while not steamrollering the palate.

Gather some friends together — ideal numbers range from just two of you to around 12, but any more can prove a little chaotic — and decide on whether you'd like your tasting to follow a theme.

If there's no theme, then ask six of those involved to each bring along a wine of their choosing — if there are fewer than six people, each person should bring two or three bottles, which might include wine from their own collection or a bottle they think would be interesting to taste blind.

Try not to choose wines that are too obscure. I can recall a blind tasting that was sprung upon me and fellow wine journalists in Greece, a country that has hundreds of indigenous grape varieties, most of which we'd never tried. While we were able to make an assessment of the character and quality of the wines, no one could even attempt a guess at what they were, which made it something of a fruitless exercise.

PICK A THEME

If you decide to follow a theme, this could range from the more general, limiting the wines bought by criteria such as price or colour to something quite specific. You could choose to recreate some of the tastings that have gone before, except this time without knowing which wine is which, or choose a completely new theme such as one that features the same grape variety or style of wine, but from different countries or regions. Or you could just select from a single region to really home in on similarities and differences and get an unbiased idea of your preferences.

For a tasting that makes you think about value for money, pick wines of a similar kind from a certain price range, or combine cheap with more expensive bottles — see if you can rank them correctly in terms of price and whether you think they're worth what's being asked for them. You could also run a tasting that pitches big brands against wines from smaller wineries and see how they stack up.

It can be fun to put in a ringer for interest, i.e. a wine from outside the theme to see if anyone spots it as an impostor in the line-up. For example, if you're tasting Cabernet Sauvignon, you could slip in a Shiraz. Or if you're doing a tasting of higher-priced wines, put in something inexpensive and see if it sticks out.

BUY AND BAG YOUR WINES

When you've decided on your theme, allocate to each person a wine to buy that fits the tasting. For example if your theme is

'Chardonnay from around the world', someone should buy a bottle from France, another from Australia, and so on.

On the night, the bottles need to be disguised. It's possible to purchase special bags for this purpose, or use the single bottle paper bags provided by many liquor stores. Number each one to avoid any confusion.

GET GUESSING

Now the real fun starts as the same wine is sampled by each taster who then has to consider the characters they're encountering in their anonymous glass of wine and think about what it might be. Encourage people to initially assess a wine in silence so they can reach their own conclusions. There's nothing like the power of suggestion to get folk toeing the same, often erroneous, line — if they'd listened to their own palate they might have made a quite different judgement.

When everyone's reached their own opinion on the wines and made some private notes, these can be shared. These will often be very different, which is all part of the fun. As well as trying to guess something like a wine's grape variety, country or region, tasters might also like to rank the wines in order of preference.

There are many clues that can be used to lead to a wine's identity. Acid tends to be higher and body lighter from cooler climates. Then there are grapes like Riesling where acid is inherently high, Pinot Noir which has a lighter body, or Cabernet Sauvignon that can have grippy tannins.

New World wines often have more upfront fruit than their

European counterparts, while older wines lose their primary fruit, with whites often becoming more toasty and reds more savoury and spicy.

There's also the character of the aromas and fruit flavours that you can cross-reference with what you remember from wines you've tried before. Sauvignon Blanc with its overly herbaceous character is often easy to spot. And if you're picking up oak, then ask yourself on what varieties does it tend to be used.

No one should be under pressure to say exactly what a wine is, but some might like to have a go at the grape variety or region. If you've picked up on a wine's vibrant cherry fruit, good acidity and notes of thyme, you may have a hunch that it is a Central Otago Pinot Noir. Only a very experienced taster could start to discern its sub-region, and you'd have to possess in-depth knowledge of a region's individual producers to be able to suggest a label — unless you had a head start by knowing what wineries were in the line-up or cheated by sneaking a look!

There's no shame in guessing incorrectly. Even professional palates can get it wrong.

THE BIG REVEAL

Ideally the great unveiling should be done after all the wines have been tasted, particularly if there's been a theme. When no theme is involved, each wine can be revealed after everyone has formed — and shared — their own opinion. The reveal is likely to result in gasps of amazement, some chin stroking and the odd satisfied smile or congratulatory cheer!

WINE OPTIONS

For those who enjoy a competitive approach, a game called Wine Options has turned blind tasting into something of a sport. In this game wines are tried by teams or individuals, who are then asked to pick a correct statement from options in a series of questions until it's narrowed down to guessing the actual wine.

Although there are those who take this quite seriously, it can be a light-hearted and entertaining way to get a dinner party going or finish off a wine-filled night.

If you're setting up your own Wine Options showdown, you ideally need an MC. This could be the host or person who has selected the wine or wines for the game in the first place. As in blind tastings, it's not fair to make ultra-eclectic wine choices; the wines chosen should be from well-known grape varieties and regions.

Some official versions of the game feature four red wines and four white wines, but there can be as few or as many wines as you feel suit the event. Decant the wines into individual jugs for anonymous pouring or serve them from bagged bottles.

The idea is that five questions are asked regarding each wine after it's poured, which start with the general, then move to the specific, with the final question suggesting some actual wines it could be. Players are given three possible answers in each case and someone from each team (or individuals as the case may be) then writes down the chosen option. The MC then asks for everyone to indicate which choice they made, after which he or she will reveal the correct answer.

In quick-fire elimination versions of the game, a person or

team has to sit out or down as soon as they get a question wrong (in some versions everyone starts standing, with the last person remaining upstanding the winner). The winner for each wine or round is the last team or player in the game.

Another way to play is to award points for each correct answer (see example opposite using a popular Sauvignon Blanc), with the scores tallied up at the end to find the winner.

This basic template can be adjusted. One alternative would be to replace the question on price with one on vintage date. An extra element of fun can be injected into the game by including humorous questions, especially towards the end.

THE LAST WORD

Keep tasting, keep your mind open to new wine experiences and you'll keep accruing the knowledge that will help you appreciate wine in all its infinite variety.

VILLA MARIA PRIVATE BIN
MARLBOROUGH SAUVIGNON BLANC
2009

QUESTION	OPTION A	OPTION B	OPTION C	ANSWER	POINTS
Is this wine predominantly:	Chardonnay	Sauvignon Blanc	Gewürztraminer	B	3
Does the wine come from:	New Zealand	Australia	France	A	4
Were the grapes grown in:	Hawke's Bay	Central Otago	Marlborough	C	4
Is the price of the wine:	$15—20	Under $15	Over $20	A	4
Is the wine labelled:	Oyster Bay Sauvignon Blanc 09	Dog Point Section 94 07	Villa Maria Private Bin 09	C	5

Recommended
Retailers

North Island

NORTHLAND

Fishbone Wine Merchants, 88 Kerikeri Road

This Kerikeri wine merchant, attached to the Fishbone Café, stocks a large selection of premium New Zealand as well as French, Italian and Australian wines.

CONTACT: 09) 407 6065/021 407 606, fishbonecafe@xtra.co.nz

OPEN: Wed–Fri 2–7pm or phone 021 407 606

NUMBER OF DIFFERENT WINES STOCKED: 400–600 changing selection

WINE TASTINGS: runs a wine club as well as being licensed as a wine bar with a range of premium wines available for tastings

AUCKLAND

Accent On Wine, 347 Parnell Road

Imports many of its interesting array of European wines direct, with a strong emphasis on wines from Bordeaux, Burgundy and the Rhône, while also carrying wines from New Zealand, Australia and often New World countries such as Argentina.

CONTACT: 09) 358 2552, aow@xtra.co.nz, sales@accentonwine.co.nz, www.accentonwine.co.nz

OPEN: Mon–Thu 10am–9.30pm, Fri 10am–10pm, Sat 11am–10pm, Sun and public holidays 11am–9pm

NUMBER OF DIFFERENT WINES STOCKED: 1500

WINE TASTINGS: three-monthly Regular Tasting Dozen (RTD) for the shop's wine society

OTHER SERVICES: delivers throughout New Zealand and to some other countries

Bacchus Cellars, 427 Remuera Road, Remuera

Bacchus prides itself in having tasted every wine on its shelves and specialises in Pinot Noir and boutique wineries in New Zealand, France, Italy, Spain, South America, South Africa and Australia.

CONTACT: 09) 520 3783, remuera@bacchuscellars.co.nz, www.bacchuscellars.co.nz

OPEN: Mon–Thu 10am–8.30pm, Fri–Sat 10am–9pm, Sun 12pm–7pm,

NUMBER OF DIFFERENT WINES STOCKED: 450–500

WINE TASTINGS: in-store tasting Friday and Saturday evenings from 4–7pm; themed wine night every second Wednesday

OTHER SERVICES: Bacchus Wine Club is free to join with members receiving discounts on every wine purchase

Caro's Wines, 114 St Georges Bay Road, Parnell

One of the best ranges of wine in the city featuring a particularly good selection of imported Spanish wines, which the Caro brothers bring in themselves.

CONTACT: 09) 377 9974, wine@caros.co.nz, www.caros.co.nz

OPEN: Mon–Fri 9am–6.30pm, Sat 9.30am–5.30pm

NUMBER OF DIFFERENT WINES STOCKED: 1000

WINE TASTINGS: hosts Bob

Campbell's wine courses as well as tastings for its wine club plus offers weekly email updates

The Fine Wine Delivery Company, 50 Cook Street, Auckland Central

Substantial family-run company with a focus on New Zealand wines as well as a sound selection of international names and a 100% money-back guarantee on all wines purchased.

CONTACT: 09) 377 2300, wine@finewinedelivery.co.nz, www.finewinedelivery.co.nz, www.bestwinebuys.co.nz

OPEN: Mon–Fri 9am–6.30pm, Sat 10.30am–5pm

NUMBER OF DIFFERENT WINES STOCKED: 2000

WINE TASTINGS: 40 wines open in store for tasting through its Enomatic tasting machines; winemaker tastings in store on Saturdays 2–3 times a month; hosts an annual Pinot road show around the country every October

OTHER SERVICES: individual temperature- and humidity-controlled wine cellars available for lease to private collectors, plus a bulk storage facility, highly informative website featuring tasting notes and weekly videos with a dedicated under $15 site

First Glass, 5 Huron Street, Takapuna

North Shore institution specialising in Chardonnay and Shiraz, that hosts one of the country's largest weekly wine tastings.

CONTACT: 09) 486 6415, firstglass@clear.net.nz, www.first-glass.co.nz

OPEN: Mon–Fri 9am–6.30pm, Sat 9am–6pm

NUMBER OF DIFFERENT WINES STOCKED: 1500

WINE TASTINGS: every Wednesday at 7pm, cost $15, no reservations necessary. Also hosts possibly the largest continuous Wine Options competition in the world. Online wine purchases can be delivered throughout the country

Glengarry Wines

New Zealand's oldest wine retailer and largest seller of premium imported wines, this family-owned chain with specially trained staff has an extensive local selection of wines, plus an increasingly impressive international fine-wine list.

FLAGSHIP STORE/VICTORIA PARK BRANCH: cnr Sale and Wellesley Streets

CONTACT: 09) 379 3740, sales@glengarry.co.nz,

www.glengarry.co.nz

OPEN: 7 days, times vary from shop to shop

NUMBER OF DIFFERENT WINES STOCKED: more than 8000

WINE TASTINGS: wines clubs at all branches; exclusive tastings offered by fine-wine team; specialist Pinot Noir and Bordeaux Clubs; monthly food and wine matching at its Dida's Food store; national online service and mail order through its monthly wine letter

OTHER SERVICES: overseas shipping, functions advice, glass hire, hire of tasting rooms, cellaring advice, brokering, *en primeur* and extensive fine-wine indents

CITY BRANCH: cnr Wellesley Street and Mayoral Drive, Auckland Central

CONTACT: 09) 379 8416, city@glengarry.co.nz

DEVONPORT BRANCH: cnr Clarence and Wynyard Streets

CONTACT: 09) 445 2989, devonport@glengarry.co.nz

HERNE BAY BRANCH: 54 Jervois Road,

CONTACT: 09) 378 8555, jervois@glengarry.co.nz

GLENGARRY NEW ZEALAND WINE MAKER'S CENTRE: cnr Elliot and

Victoria Streets, Auckland Central. The National Bank Centre, 205–225 Queen Street, Auckland
CONTACT: 09) 379 5858, info@nzwinemakerscentre.co.nz

KINGSLAND BRANCH:
467 New North Road
CONTACT: 09) 815 9207, kingsland@glengarry.co.nz

MISSION BAY BRANCH:
49 Tamaki Drive
CONTACT: 09) 528 5272, missionbay@glengarry.co.nz

MT EDEN BRANCH:
250 Dominion Road
CONTACT: 09) 623 0811, dominion@glengarry.co.nz

NEWMARKET BRANCH:
22 Morrow Street
CONTACT: 09) 524 5789, newmarket@glengarry.co.nz

PARNELL BRANCH: 164 Parnell Road
CONTACT: 09) 358 1333, parnell@glengarry.co.nz

PONSONBY BRANCH:
139 Ponsonby Road
CONTACT: 09) 378 8252, ponsonby@glengarry.co.nz

REMUERA BRANCH:
400 Remuera Road
CONTACT: 09) 523 1594, remuera@glengarry.co.nz

TAKAPUNA BRANCH: cnr Killarney Street and Hurstmere Road
CONTACT: 09) 486 1770, takapuna@glengarry.co.nz

WESTMERE BRANCH:
164 Garnet Road
CONTACT: 09) 360 4035, westmere@glengarry.co.nz

La Vino Wines & Spirits, 16 Williamson Avenue, Ponsonby

An expansive shop with a wide range of New Zealand wines, including many hard-to-get labels, as well as imports and a good selection of organic wines.
CONTACT: 09) 360 0134, wines@lavino.co.nz, www.lavino.co.nz
OPEN: Mon– Thurs 9.30am–10pm, Fri–Sat 9.30am–11pm, Sunday 12pm–9pm, public holidays 12pm–8pm
WINE TASTINGS: mostly on Friday and/or Saturday afternoons from 3pm
OTHER SERVICES: discounts through membership of La Vino Wine Club, plus 'members only' offers

Maison Vauron French Wine Merchant, 5 McColl Street, Newmarket

From everyday Vin de Pays to the greatest Grands Crus, Maison Vauron is a one-stop shop for Francophile wine drinkers with over 220 French producers represented.
CONTACT: 09) 529 0157, jc@mvauron.co.nz, www.mvauron.co.nz
OPEN: Mon–Sat 8.30am–6.30pm
NUMBER OF DIFFERENT WINES STOCKED: more than 2500
WINE TASTINGS: monthly themed tastings at shop; plus corporate and private wine-tasting events

Milford Cellars, 172A Kitchener Road, Milford

Independent shop with its main focus on New Zealand and single vineyard wines, plus an extensive Australian selection and a smattering from elsewhere in the world.
CONTACT: 09) 486 1977, fax: 09) 486 1978, milford.cellars@xtra.co.nz
OPEN: Mon–Sat 10am–8pm, Sun 3.30–7pm
WINE TASTINGS: scheduled tastings held
OTHER SERVICES: monthly email newsletter

Millar & Co/St Heliers Bay Wines, 419 Tamaki Drive, St Heliers

With over three decades behind it, this establishment offers wines from $10 to $2000 across its large range that spans local labels to those from Australia, South Africa, South America, France, Spain, Italy and even Croatia.

CONTACT: 09) 575 9293, sales@millar.co.nz, www.millar.co.nz, www.stheliersbaywines.com
OPEN: Mon 10am–8pm, Tues–Thurs 10am–9pm, Fri–Sat 10am–10pm, Sun and public holidays 12–8pm
NUMBER OF DIFFERENT WINES STOCKED: more than 600
WINE TASTINGS: free tastings of eight different wines a week from its in-house wine-preserving Winestation machine, in-store tastings once a month, regular wine club functions
OTHER SERVICES OFFERED: free delivery throughout New Zealand for orders over $200; delivery arranged to the US, UK, Australia, Japan and Hong Kong

Peter Maude Fine Wines, 33 Coates Avenue, Orakei

Very possibly boasting the best range of Burgundy in the Southern Hemisphere, French fine-wine expert Peter Maude is the man to talk to about top wine, including Bordeaux *en primeur.*

CONTACT: 09) 520 3023, petermaude@pmfw.co.nz, www.pmfw.co.nz
OPEN: Mon–Sat 10am–8pm
NUMBER OF DIFFERENT WINES STOCKED: approximately 200
WINE TASTINGS: annual dinner tastings led by some of France's leading winemakers

Point Wines, 141 Queen Street, Northcote Point

A supporter of small and medium-sized vineyards around New Zealand with a sizeable selection of international wines.

CONTACT: 09) 480 6463, orders@pointwines.co.nz, www.pointwines.co.nz
OPEN: Mon–Tues 11am–7pm, Wed–Sat 11am–8pm, Sun 2–7pm
NUMBER OF DIFFERENT WINES STOCKED: approximately 800
WINE TASTINGS: themed monthly evening tastings in store; festival days; winemaker evenings; wine options; blind-tasting nights; tailored corporate tastings
OTHER SERVICES: tailor-made wine plans with a personally selected case of wine delivered free to Auckland metropolitan customers on a frequency and budget to suit; wine bar soon to open at premises.

The Village Winery, 417 Mt Eden Road, Mt Eden Village

While originally starting out as a working winery back in 1994, The Village Winery's main focus is now on selling wines, stocking a selection from most of the main wine producing regions of the world.

CONTACT: 09) 638 9780, shop@villagewinery.co.nz, www.villagewinery.co.nz
OPEN: Mon–Sun 1–8pm
NUMBER OF DIFFERENT WINES STOCKED: more than 1000
WINE TASTINGS: informal in-store weekly tastings, and monthly tutored tastings
OTHER SERVICES OFFERED: mail-order service via website, orders for functions

Waiheke Wine Centre, 153 Oceanview Road, Oneroa, Waiheke Island

Boasting the most extensive range of Waiheke wines in the world, this shop also carries a wide range from other New Zealand regions, as well as

sections dedicated to organic wines and other winegrowing nations.
CONTACT: 09) 372 6139, fax: 09) 372 5031, info@waihekewinecentre.co.nz, www.waihekewinecentre.co.nz
OPEN: Mon–Thurs 9.30am–7.30pm, Fri–Sat 9.30am–8.30pm, Sun 11am–5pm
TASTINGS: features *Cuisine* Top Ten wine tastings with food matches from top chefs held in local vineyards plus tastings in-store with local winemakers; international themes and blind tastings; wine club
OTHER SERVICES: free chilled delivery on Waiheke and free around New Zealand ($10 for rural deliveries), also exports around the world

Wine Circle, Shop 2, 329A SH16, Huapai

A gem of a shop run by occasional wine scribe Chris Carrad, importing and stocking an exciting and eclectic selection of wines from around the world and even preservative-free examples.
CONTACT: 09) 412 2258, winecircle@xtra.co.nz
OPEN: Mon–Sat 10am–8pm, Sun 11am–7pm
NUMBER OF DIFFERENT WINES STOCKED: 1200
WINE TASTINGS: monthly wine club

Wine Direct, 16 St Marks Road, Newmarket

A European wine emporium whose adventurous range covers most price brackets, with a particularly comprehensive offering from France and Italy, an extensive choice of German and Austrian wines, as well as interesting wines gathered from across the globe.
CONTACT: 09) 529 5267, sales@winedirect.co.nz, www.winedirect.co.nz
OPEN: Mon–Fri 9am–6pm, Sat 10am–4pm
NUMBER OF DIFFERENT WINES STOCKED: more than 1000
WINE TASTINGS: regular in-store tastings

The Wine Vault, 453 Richmond Road, Grey Lynn

As well as a comprehensive selection of Pinot Noir and Champagne, this shop also stocks a large range of wines from all of the major and some of the lesser-known regions of both the Old and New Worlds.
CONTACT: 09) 376 3520, orders@thewinevault.co.nz, www.thewinevault.co.nz
OPEN: Daily 11am–8pm

NUMBER OF DIFFERENT WINES STOCKED: more than 1000
WINE TASTINGS: monthly wine tastings
OTHER SERVICES: runs a French language and wine school, plus the Wine Vault wine academy

HAMILTON

The Hamilton Wine Company, 29 Hood Street

With one of the best wine selections in the Waikato, this shop's major strength is sourcing wines from the interesting smaller wineries of New Zealand and Australia.
CONTACT: 07) 839 1190, www.hamiltonwine.co.nz
OPEN: Mon–Wed 10am–6pm, Thurs–Sat 10am–7pm,
NUMBER OF DIFFERENT WINES STOCKED: 1000+
WINE TASTINGS: every Saturday 12–4pm

Hillcrest Fine Wines Ltd, 31 Cambridge Road, Hillcrest

A small retailer stocking boutique producers and hard-to-find wines.
CONTACT: 07) 856 6739/021 741 852, fax: 07) 856 6730, info@hillcrestfinewines.co.nz,

www.hillcrestfinewines.co.nz

OPEN: Mon 11am–7pm, Tues–Wed 11am–7.30pm, Thurs–Sat 11am–8pm, Sun 11am–5pm

NUMBER OF DIFFERENT WINES STOCKED: 350

WINE TASTINGS: seated monthly tastings, plus an open tasting every two months

OTHER SERVICES OFFERED: free delivery within Hamilton; will freight anywhere in New Zealand

Primo Vino, 955 Victoria Street

'Wine is fun; drink what you enjoy with a desire to try something new,' advise the folk at this Hamilton wine shop where the emphasis is on Australasian wines.

CONTACT: 07) 839 3139, wine@primovino.co.nz, www.primovino.co.nz

OPEN: Mon–Fri 10am–6pm, Sat 10am–4pm

NUMBER OF DIFFERENT WINES STOCKED: 300–400

WINE TASTINGS: Friday 4.30–6pm at least twice a month; monthly wine club/educational tasting

CAMBRIDGE
Cambridge Wine Co Ltd, 72b Victoria Street

A boutique wine shop specialising in smaller, quality-focused New Zealand producers and with a good range of Australian reds.

CONTACT: 07) 827 5123, sales@cambridgewine.co.nz, www.cambridgewine.co.nz

OPEN: Mon–Tues 11am–5.30pm, Wed–Fri 10am–6pm, Sat 10am–4pm

WINE TASTINGS: occasional

KATIKATI
Finer Wines, 8 Main Road

Fine and rare wines are the focus of this establishment, which stocks numerous top Australasian examples, as well as a wide range of Châteauneuf-du-Pape, Sauternes and vintage port, plus wines from across Europe and the New World, including many aged examples.

CONTACT: 07) 549 3463, finerwines@xtra.co.nz

OPEN: Mon–Fri 10am–5.30pm, Sat 10am–2.30pm

NUMBER OF DIFFERENT WINES STOCKED: 1800

WINE TASTINGS: monthly themed tastings in shop cellar

OTHER SERVICES: Finer Wines Wine

Club featuring selected wines based on customer preferences; will ship internationally

TAURANGA
Hillsdene Wines, 673 Cameron Road

A business with over five decades of experience supplying the Bay of Plenty with wines from a comprehensive range that's largely focused on homegrown examples.

CONTACT: 07) 578 7236, info@hillsdenewines.co.nz, www.hillsdenewines.co.nz

OPEN: Mon 9am–8pm, Tues 9am–8.30pm, Wed–Sat 9am–9pm, Sun 11am–7pm (8pm in summer)

NUMBER OF DIFFERENT WINES STOCKED: more than 2000

WINE TASTINGS: in-store Wine Club every six weeks, plus general tastings throughout the year

OTHER SERVICES: gift baskets

TE PUKE
McGregors, 120 Jellicoe Street

A family-owned store with over 40 years in the business, McGregors offers a wide selection of predominantly local and some imported wines, specialising in older bottles.

CONTACT: 07) 573 7570, sales@mcgregors-wines.co.nz, www.mcgregors-wines.co.nz

OPEN: Monday 9am–6pm, Tues–Wed 9am–7.30pm, Thurs 9am–8pm, Fri–Sat 9am–9pm, Sun 10–6pm

NUMBER OF DIFFERENT WINES STOCKED: more than 1000

ROTORUA
Arawa Fine Wines, 1106 Tutanekai Street

Boutique wines not available in the supermarkets are the focus of this small Rotorua shop.

CONTACT: 07) 348 6590, arawafinewines@xtra.co.nz

OPEN: Daily 11am–9.30pm

NUMBER OF DIFFERENT WINES STOCKED: more than 100

WINE TASTINGS: monthly in-store, usually on the second Thursday of the month

TAUPO
The Merchant of Taupo, 114 Spa Road

Happy to source specific local wines for its customers, the Merchant of Taupo specialises in wines from throughout New Zealand.

CONTACT: 07) 378 4626, info@themerchant.co.nz, www.themerchant.co.nz

OPEN: Mon–Fri 9am–6pm, Sat 9am–5pm

NUMBER OF DIFFERENT WINES STOCKED: more than 600

WINE TASTINGS: in-store tastings from 3.30–6pm every Friday featuring a wine of the week and/or food of the week; annual Wine & Food Expo in July featuring local and imported wines

Scenic Cellars, 32 Roberts Street

A lakeside shop boasting New Zealand's largest underground retail wine cellar with an impressive range of local wines and from most of the major wine regions of the world, Bordeaux in particular.

CONTACT: 07) 378 5704, info@sceniccellars.co.nz, www.sceniccellars.co.nz

OPEN: Daily 9am–7pm (extended hours in summer)

NUMBER OF DIFFERENT WINES STOCKED: 3000

WINE TASTINGS: 1–2 per month; themed Cellar Dinners throughout the year

OTHER SERVICES: wine-tasting events and wine-options games

HAWKE'S BAY/ HAVELOCK NORTH
Advintage, 4 Donnelly Street

One of the country's largest wine stores with a leaning towards Australasian wines under $25, but also boasting a substantial fine-wine section.

CONTACT: 0800 111 660, orders@advintage.co.nz, www.advintage.co.nz

OPEN: Mon–Fri 9am–5.30pm, Sat 10am–5pm

NUMBER OF DIFFERENT WINES STOCKED: 1500

WINE TASTINGS: monthly structured paying fine-wine tastings in stand-alone tasting room; informal free tastings several times each year featuring 30–40 wines

OTHER SERVICES: tailor-made case buying-plan service allowing clients to choose favourite wine styles, price points, delivery frequency

PALMERSTON NORTH

The Village Wine Trader, 350 Albert St

Palmerston North's only specialist wine shop.

CONTACT: 06) 357 0779, wine.trader@xtra.co.nz, www.winetrader.co.nz

OPEN: Mon–Wed 10am–7pm, Thurs–Sat 10am–8pm, Sun 2–6pm

WINE TASTINGS: monthly in-store

WELLINGTON

Glengarry (see Auckland section for main entry)

THORNDON QUAY BRANCH:

232 Thorndon Quay

CONTACT: 04) 472 7051, thorndon@glengarry.co.nz

KELBURN BRANCH: 85 Upland Road

CONTACT: 04) 475 7849, kelburn@glengarry.co.nz

COURTENAY PLACE BRANCH:

Paramount Cinema Building, 27 Courtenay Place

CONTACT: 04) 385 9600, courtenay@glengarry.co.nz

Regional Wines & Spirits, 15 Ellice Street, Basin Reserve

Great wine store with enthusiastic and knowledgeable staff offering an exciting and broad range of wines from New Zealand and beyond.

CONTACT: 04) 385 6952, wine@regionalwines.co.nz, www.regionalwines.co.nz

OPEN: Mon–Sat 9am–10pm, Sun 11am–7.30pm

NUMBER OF DIFFERENT WINES STOCKED: more than 4500

WINE TASTINGS: intensive tasting programme held at store; wine and food events in conjunction with local restaurants, Bob Campbell MW wine courses

Rumbles, 32 Waring Taylor Street

Describing themselves as 'international nice wine specialists regardless of brand or fad', Rumbles stocks a sizable selection of more eclectic wines.

CONTACT: 04) 472 7045, fax: 04) 472 7675, info@rumbles.co.nz, www.rumbles.co.nz

OPEN: Mon–Fri 9am–7pm, Sat 10am–5pm

NUMBER OF DIFFERENT WINES STOCKED: approximately 1000

WINE TASTINGS: in-store tastings most Fridays; customer tastings once or twice a month

OTHER SERVICES: The Durif Club for fine- and rare-wine enthusiasts

Wineseeker, 86–96 Victoria Street

Innovative and well set-out central city store that 'loves to match people with wine', selling unique and boutique wines from around the world.

CONTACT: 04) 473 0228, wine@wineseeker.co.nz, www.wineseeker.co.nz

OPEN: Mon–Wed 10am–7pm, Thurs–Fri 10am–8pm, Sat 11am–6pm

WINE TASTINGS: in-store every day; two-monthly food and wine matching courses with restaurants; monthly wine appreciation course; monthly specialty tasting; feature vineyard tasting in-store by winemaker; plus other wine-tasting evenings throughout the year, including speed dating wine evenings, gay and lesbian wine evenings

South Island

NELSON
Casa del Vino, 214 Hardy Street

A treasure trove of local and international fine wines run by the brother-and-sister team of Ann and Mark Banks, who have developed vineyards here in New Zealand as well as building up knowledge through their regular travels to many of the world's wine regions.

CONTACT: 03) 548 0088, wine@casadelvino.co.nz, www.casadelvino.co.nz
OPEN: Mon–Sat 10am–6pm
NUMBER OF DIFFERENT WINES STOCKED: more than 1000
WINE TASTINGS: wine club; free Saturday tastings in-store; formal monthly in-store evening tastings
OTHER SERVICES: worldwide shipping service available, gift boxes and free cards

HOKITIKA
West Coast Wine Company, 108 Revell Street

Enthusiastically run wine shop and bar specialising in smaller wineries from New Zealand, Australia and Europe.
CONTACT: 03) 755 5417, colette@westcoastwine.co.nz
OPEN: Mon–Sat 9.30am–late
WINE TASTINGS: occasional with visiting winemakers and merchants

CHRISTCHURCH
Decant, 61 Mandeville St, Riccarton

An exciting new addition to Christchurch's wine scene, this Euro-focused wine store and French-style café has New Zealand's largest range of top German Rieslings, as well as a titillating selection of great French, Italian, Spanish and selected Australasian wines.
CONTACT: 03) 343 1945, decant@decantwine.co.nz, www.decantwine.co.nz

OPEN: Mon–Fri 9am–6pm, Sat 9am–5pm
NUMBER OF DIFFERENT WINES STOCKED: 1500
WINE TASTINGS: held most weeks including premium European tastings and those hosted by visiting winemakers
OTHER SERVICES: French language lessons with wine and cheese; educational wine classes; free local delivery

The Grape Escape, 69 Centaurus Road

Local liquor store offering a small range of wines including bin-end bargains and older bottles.
CONTACT: 03) 332 0233
OPEN: Mon–Fri 11am–7.15pm, Sat 11am–8.15pm
NUMBER OF DIFFERENT WINES STOCKED: 200
WINE TASTING: every second Monday at 6pm

Hemingway Fine Wines, Cnr Durham Street North and Chester Street West

A large range of interesting local wines as well as a strong international selection from France, Spain and Italy.
CONTACT: 03) 374 3344,
hemingwayfinewines@xtra.co.nz,
www.hemingwayfinewines.co.nz
OPEN: Mon–Sat 10am–7pm
NUMBER OF DIFFERENT WINES STOCKED: more than 1000
WINE TASTINGS: every two to three weeks

Vino Fino, 188 Durham Street South, Christchurch Central

The South Island's largest single retailer of wine that's sourced from both artisan producers and the big names, with well-priced New Zealand wines the mainstay of the business, which also encompasses a solid range of Australian and European labels.
CONTACT: 03) 365 5134,
wine@vinofino.co.nz,
www.vinofino.co.nz
OPEN: Mon–Sat 9am–6pm
NUMBER OF DIFFERENT WINES STOCKED: 2500
WINE TASTINGS: Tuesday evenings at the shop, with themes and visiting winemakers; twice yearly wine festival

OTHER SERVICES: wine club providing specialised newsletters and a discount card

The Wine Ferret, 130C Montreal Street

Somewhat off the beaten track, this tiny shop similarly specialises in non-mainstream wines from around the world, the majority of which they import themselves.
CONTACT: 03) 379 1674,
ldick@se.co.nz,
www.wineferret.co.nz
OPEN: Mon–Fri 12.30pm–4pm,
Sat 12–5pm
NUMBER OF DIFFERENT WINES STOCKED: 500
WINE TASTINGS: every two weeks, wines matched with regional food

DUNEDIN

Castle Macadam Wine, 11 Mailer Street, Mornington

A small shop specialising in small New Zealand producers and wines that are not available in the supermarkets.
CONTACT: 03) 453 3327,
darren@nzwinespecialist.co.nz,
www.nzwinespecialist.co.nz
OPEN: Tues–Sat 2pm–7pm

NUMBER OF DIFFERENT WINES STOCKED: 250

Meenan Wines & Spirits, 750 Great King Street

Meenans has been an importing wholesaler since the 1860s and now stocks a wide array of wines spanning the world's wine regions from Central Otago to Morocco.
CONTACT: 03) 477 2047,
orders@meenans.co.nz,
www.meenans.co.nz
OPEN: Mon–Thu 9am–6pm,
Fri–Sat 9am–7pm
NUMBER OF DIFFERENT WINES STOCKED: 1400
WINE TASTINGS: by request

Munslow's Fine Wines, 338 George Street

Central Otago is one of Munslow's main focuses, as well as small exclusive labels from throughout the country, plus Dunedin's most extensive selection of international wines.
CONTACT: 03) 477 1585,
fax: 03) 477 1785,
munslowswines@paradise.net.nz
OPEN: Mon–Wed 10am–7pm,
Thurs 10am–8pm, Fri 10am–9pm,
Sat 10am–8pm
NUMBER OF DIFFERENT WINES

STOCKED: 900–1000

WINE TASTINGS: in-store fortnightly, generally involving a winemaker or winery owner/s; specialist master classes; casual Friday at Five tasting of new wines in-store

OTHER SERVICES: strong wine club with a weekly email newsletter; several Introduction to Wine courses each year

QUEENSTOWN
Wine Tastes: Central Otago Wine Experience, 14 Beach Street

New Zealand Pinot Noir, from the area as well as the best national players, is Wine Tastes' main area of expertise, a couple of dozen of which are always available for tasting in-store.

CONTACT: 03) 409 2226, queenstown@winetastes.com, www.winetastes.com

OPEN: Daily 10am–10pm

NUMBER OF DIFFERENT WINES STOCKED: 850

WINE TASTINGS: self-service with over 80 wines available for tasting every day in the shop's Enomatic machine; informal afternoon tastings often with local winemakers; wine club events held in store throughout the year

WANAKA
Wanaka Fine Wines, 19 Helwick Street

Wanaka shop with many years of industry experience specialising in the local Central Otago wines.

CONTACT: 03) 443 7539, wines@wanakafinewines.co.nz, www.centralotagopinot.co.nz or www.wanakafinewines.co.nz (coming soon)

OPEN: Mon–Sat 9am–9pm, Sun 10.30am–8.30pm

NUMBER OF DIFFERENT WINES STOCKED: 1000

WINE TASTINGS: some *Cuisine* magazine tastings; winter in-store tastings from local wineries

Online, at Auction, Specialists

E-TAILERS

WWW.BLACKMARKET.CO.NZ:
bargain-busting site selling many
good-value special labels and surplus
stock from New Zealand wineries

WWW.GOLDMEDALWINES.CO.NZ
Chilean specialist selling some of the
best names available in New Zealand..

WWW.NZ-WINE-SOCIETY.CO.NZ:
organisation offering by-the-case wine
plans for different budgets

WWW.PLANETWINE.CO.NZ
Wine importer site selling to the
general public, with the country's
most comprehensive selection of
South African wine.

WWW.TRUEWINES.CO.NZ:
online operation selling full-price New
Zealand wines

WWW.WINEIMPORTER.CO.NZ:
offers an excellent selection of
predominantly European wines from
keenly priced quaffers to top drops

WWW.WINESALE.CO.NZ:
online wine store created after the
purchase of cut-price wine retailer
Corporate Direct, still full of sharp deals

AUCTION HOUSES

Dunbar Sloane

General auction house that runs three
to four fine-wine auctions featuring
local and international wines.
WELLINGTON: 04) 472 1367,
wine@dunbarsloane.co.nz,
www.dunbarsloane.com

Fitzgerald Wine Auctions

Specialist wine auction site with regular
auctions of current and older vintages

from New Zealand and beyond.
CONTACT: www.fitzgeraldwine.co.nz

Webbs, 18 Manukau Road, Newmarket, Auckland

Auction house with specialist fine-
wine department holding eight sales
annually of fine, collectable wine from
around the world.
CONTACT: 09) 524 6804,
auctions@webbs.co.nz,
www.webbs.co.nz

AGED WINE SPECIALISTS

Batchelor Fine and Rare Wines

Private client traders specialising in
older vintages
CONTACT: 021 889 084,
luke@batchelorwines.com,
www.batchelorwines.com

Thanks

**Kemp Rare Wines, 143
Carlton Gore Road,
Newmarket**

As well as working as a distributer
for a number of New Zealand and
Australian wineries, Kemp Rare Wines
also boasts a good back catalogue of
older vintages.

CONTACT: 0800 KEMPWINE
or 09) 529 0935,
enquiries@kemprarewines.co.nz,
www.kemprarewines.co.nz

With thanks to David Khan, Helen
Greenfield, Adrian Harrison, Tony Bish,
Mike Eaton, Amanda Linnell and the
New Zealand Herald, Jo and Ross Seagar,
Negociants, and the many others
who have so generously shared their
passion, knowledge and wines with
me during the writing of this book and
throughout my travels in wine so far.

Jo Burzynska
April 2009

Index